Senator Bollweevil, Cat Extraordinaire

A Memoir

Senator Bollweevil, Cat Extraordinaire

A Memoir

Anita H. Lenssen

NOTE: $2.00 of the cost of this book will be donated to the North Carolina Society for the Prevention of Cruelty to Animals.

Published by:
Scuttlebutt Press
50 Westchester Dr.
Asheville, NC 28803-2255

In conjunction with:
Old Mountain Press, Inc.
85 John Allman Ln.
Sylva, NC 28779

www.OldMountainPress.com
Old Mountain Press eBook Division
www.oldmp.com/e-book

Copyright © 2017 Anita H. Lenssen
Interior text design by Tom Davis
Illustrated by Anita H. Lenssen
Cover Design by Jaci Moos
ISBN: 978-0-9989373-0-4
Library of Congress Control Number: 2017912405

Senator Bollweevil, Cat Extraordinaire: A Memoir.
All rights reserved. Except for brief excerpts used in reviews, no portion of this work may be reproduced or published without express written permission from the author or the author's agent.

First Edition
Printed and bound in the United States of America by Old Mountain Press
www.OldMountainPress.com • 910.476.2542
10 9 8 7 6 5 4 3 2 1

THIS BOOK IS dedicated to all veterinarians; men and women, past and present, at home or abroad, who through research and application work to prevent disease and pestilence, thereby making the world a safer environment for animals and humans alike.

And to my grandmother, Anita R. Coxe; her way with all creatures taught me the true meaning of animal magnetism.

And most of all to Senator Bollweevil, who let me tell his story.

A. H. L.

Acknowledgments

WRITING A BOOK with the intention of having it published requires the assistance of a variety of dedicated folks who share the burden of making it right. To those dedicated caregivers and friends, I owe deep and profound thanks and appreciation for the many hours they devoted to correcting typos, grammar errors, spelling, and continuity. Garnell and David Jackson stole many hours from their already jam-packed agendas to read and reread every word, phrase, sentence, paragraph, and chapter; my undying gratitude to them for their diligence. And, well-deserved accolades to Susan Snowden, Snowden Editorial Services, who tackled the monumental task of editing the final copy assuring it was ready for print. And also to Tom Davis of Old Mountain Press for walking me through the publishing process.

A very special thanks to Dr. Douglas Elledge, DVM, Redwood Animal Hospital, for checking the content and usage of the veterinary terms and information scattered throughout the book. There are no words to describe my gratitude to Dr. Keith Allan, MVS, MS, Upstate Veterinary Specialists surgeon, for the incredibly delicate job he did removing the cyst in my throat and giving me a new lease on life.

Kudos to Caroline Shelley for all her encouragement and for providing assorted new bow-ties and formal wear for my pictures; she made me look the Southern-bred statesman that I have always aspired to be; to Larry Duckett, whose lap provided a perfect cat-napping spot in between my creative endeavors; to Mahala Ernest for sharing her vast knowledge of our neighborhood and for providing a loving sanctuary for the numerous felines that have crossed her path through the years;

to Miss G's daughter for caring enough to send me to a specialist for my throat surgery. I would not be here today were it not for her.

Grateful meows to my beta readers: Agnes, Barbara, Bobbye, David, and Keith for their invaluable feedback.

And last but not least, purrs, head bumps, and leg rubs to Anita H. Lenssen, my confidant, ghostwriter, typist, and backer, who believed enough in me and my story to put it on paper for me.

S. B.

CONTENTS

Chapter 1 1
   Family Affairs
Chapter 2 9
   Things Happen
Chapter 3 15
   First Things First
Chapter 4 19
   Fuzzbucket
Chapter 5 23
   Gabby
Chapter 6 29
   For Whom the Bells Toll
Chapter 7 33
   Masked Marauders
Chapter 8 41
   A New Name
Chapter 9 45
   A Stranger in Our Midst
Chapter 10 51
   The Shocking Truth
Chapter 11 57
   Ferals Beget Ferals
Chapter 12 65
   Brave Heart
Chapter 13 75
   Furever Friends
Chapter 14 81
   Homeward Bound
Chapter 15 85
   Here Today and Gone Tomorrow
Chapter 16 93
   Inherent Danger

Chapter 17 99
    What's in a Name?
Chapter 18 103
    Don't Get Caught Singing the Blues
Chapter 19 111
    Lifesavers Come in All Shapes
Epilogue 117

Chapter 1

Family Affairs

WHY IN THE WORLD would anyone want to read a book penned by a cat? you ask. Because it's full of lessons to be learned by cat owners and future cat owners alike. Who better to tell why a cat does what it does than a cat?

My Story

Near as I can remember, I was born under the floored portion of the garage behind the Tudor house in our middle-class neighborhood. Mom kept my brother and sisters and me there until our eyes were open and we could scamper about. Mom was well versed in the art of raising kittens, having birthed several litters prior to mine. She insisted that we mind her warnings to the last meow as she was acutely aware of the inherent dangers all around: the dog next door, the family of foxes in the woods behind the house, not to mention the black bears or occasional coyote that might wander through.

Mom was very brave and had hissed and spit and scratched several noses in her time, but she was a little cat and not a youngster anymore. I knew instinctively that she would protect us with all she had; the trick was not to put her in that position. Trying to be good all the time was a real challenge, and the four of us were bound to try her patience.

Our owners were kind, providing food and fresh water daily, but, I know now, they were not very knowledgeable about our health issues. Case in point was the number of litters they had allowed Mom to have without ever having visited a veterinarian. Many kittens had died because of a lack of immunizations, worming, or flea treatment. I think the ones that did survive had been given away to folks who did provide kitten wellness care by their veterinarian, but I really can't say for sure as I have never met any of my half-siblings to ask them.

One day when I was about four months old, signs appeared all over our neighborhood. Mom was curious but couldn't read them. It was only when she ran into an old flame of hers that she learned what they were about. He had overheard his owners talking one evening at dinner about a law that had been passed requiring all intact domestic cats and dogs, not currently in a purebred breeding situation, to be spayed or neutered immediately. That meant our whole family, Mom included. Mom tried to explain what she had heard to us, but as she didn't really understand it herself, it wasn't clear. Certainly not to me; I was much more interested in what the brilliant blue butterfly I had been stalking was going to do next.

Two days later I got a rude awakening; when offered a tasty plate of tuna, I was snatched up with nary a bite, shoved into a cardboard box with my brother, and whisked away into a car. It was the very same car that Mom had forbidden us to be in or around. I protested loudly, as did my brother. Mom and sisters were in another box beside us in the car. They were so intimidated by our cries they didn't make a sound. There were no consoling meows from Mom; very disconcerting!

Our total trip was not too long, but to me it seemed like an eternity. Soon our box was transported into a starkly bright, smelly building. I will never forget that smell and to this day dislike it intensely. Looking around through the air holes cut into the box I discovered our owners were discussing our former health issues and immunizations with a man in a white coat. None of us were up to date on anything.

"We had no idea that the feline distemper-combo and the feline leukemia vaccines should be given yearly," I overheard our owners admit.

Listening to the conversation, I learned that rabies shots are required by law to be given on a yearly basis in areas of high incidence. In areas where it is less prevalent, after the first shot is given, a booster is given one year later, followed by boosters every three years.

Lowering his head to look our owners directly in the eye, the veterinarian stated matter-of-factly, "Rabies is one of the world's most feared viruses and can be transferred from infected animals to humans. Without proper treatment, it's almost always fatal. Transferred through the saliva from the infected animal, usually through a bite, it attacks the brain and central nervous system."

He must have sensed that he had their full attention, as he continued. "There are two types of rabies, furious rabies (where the infected animal foams at the mouth and shows extreme aggression toward anyone or anything that is near) and dumb rabies (where the infected animal stumbles around and usually has trouble eating or drinking). Infection from dumb rabies is usually caused by a person or another animal getting infected saliva into an open sore or wound. That alone is a good reason to always wear gloves when handling dead animals of unknown origin. Since the early 1980s, more cats than dogs have been documented to have had rabies. Now most states require rabies shots for all domestic cats as well as dogs."

It would be years before I had any inkling of what all the "shot talk" really meant.

Before the feline leukemia vaccine could be given, a test was required to determine if any of us had the disease or were carriers. We all, including Mom, needed worming and flea treatment because she was such a good provider of mice and voles for us to play with and then eat. Mice and voles are known carriers of both worms and fleas. I can assure you that the phrase "don't play with your food" never pertained to cats and kittens. How else were we to learn to provide for ourselves if times got tough?

It was determined that the rabies vaccine and the feline leukemia test would be given before surgery.

At my tender young kittenhood age, I could comprehend only so much of the conversation. I had stopped trying to understand what it all meant at "a test was required to determine . . ." So I just pushed tighter against my brother and tried very hard not to appear worried. Suddenly a hand grasped me by the back of my neck and pulled me out of the box. Before I knew what was happening, my ears were probed, my mouth pried open, and some cold, hard stick was poked up the bunghole under my tail. I tried to jump free, but the hand that held me by the scruff of my neck was as skilled at holding me as Mom had been when she moved us as tiny kittens—from a not so secure place to a place better suited for raising a litter.

Another white-coated person joined the first one and gently but firmly tilted my head back and to the side. That was when the noisy black thing touched me on the side of my neck. If I had not been held so securely, I would have left the room right then, but I couldn't move. The fur flew anyway as the clippers vibrated against my neck. People call it shaving; a lot of men do it daily, but in my opinion, no self-respecting cat should ever have it done. Immediately the tech washed the clipped area with something that was cold, wet, and smelled awful.

I was ready to do battle right then when something stung me on the neck. Mom told me later that it was the prick from the needle they used to draw my blood for the feline leukemia test, but I wasn't convinced. It sure felt like the sting I got when I stuck my nose up to the yellow and black insect that buzzed so loudly when I slapped it with my paw. I learned a quick lesson on where not to stick my nose.

No sooner than the needle was removed from my neck—while a finger was pressed against the site to stop the flow of blood—I felt a sting again; it was on my upper thigh from the rabies shot. Shaken and a bit disoriented, I was returned to the safety of the box by myself. My brother had already been removed and was receiving all the prodding and probing that I had not enjoyed. His blood drawn and shot given, he was returned to the box with me. The same routine was repeated for Mom and each of my sisters.

Approximately twenty minutes later the veterinarian reappeared with a smile on his face. He told our owners that all the feline leukemia tests were negative and we could go on to surgery.

"You can leave now and come back this afternoon around three to pick up the two male kittens," he said. "The females need to stay overnight so we can assess their condition in the morning. We'll give the other vaccinations in ten days when you come back for us to remove the stitches or staples. We'll treat them for fleas and ticks when they're ready to go home."

Time marched on, but soon it was our slated time for surgery. My brother and I were first because our procedure could be done relatively quickly and our recovery would be shorter than Mom's or my sisters'. The last thing I remember other than the cold, hard table was the round plastic thing they shoved over my nose . . . Then I was shaking my head trying to wake up. I didn't know where I was, but I knew I was all alone. In desperation, I mewed softly but was met only with silence. As I regained a semblance of awareness, I listened to the hustle bustle in my immediate area, then dozed again. When I woke up the next time, I realized I was starved! I hadn't eaten anything since the night before.

When our owners came to pick us up that afternoon, I was removed from the recovery area crate to the plastic pet carrier they had purchased to transport us home. It had holes and a wire gate for air flow and access. As I was put into the carrier, I discovered that my brother was already there and he looked as sleepy as I was. We had matching wet spots on the back of our necks that sure smelled funny.

The receptionist told our owners we'd already been treated for fleas and ticks. "They're ready to go home," she said, "but the mother and the female kittens need to stay overnight. You can pick them up tomorrow morning between eight and nine.

"Keep an eye on them for several days. Particularly watch for swelling or drainage at the surgery site and make sure the incision stays clean so it can heal properly. Call if you have any questions or doubts."

They paid the bill, and before you could say scat, we were in the car and on our way home, without Mom! Whatever were we to do?

Eat! A plate of food was waiting when we came out of the carrier. Oh, joy! It was my favorite: chicken and liver pate! Both of us were ravenous, so we chowed down. Licking my whiskers and washing my face with my paw, I made sure I had gotten every last bite and was properly clean before I stretched out in a pool of sunshine on the porch rug. The earlier events of the day temporarily forgotten, I decided that my life was all in all pretty good.

Mom and my sisters returned the next day. Ordinarily, they would have been keen for a game of catch the mouse or hide and pounce, but it was quite apparent they just wanted to curl up and be very quiet. I had overheard our owners discussing the veterinarian's explanation that "incision" for the girls meant a small hole cut in their belly. Through it, he would remove the uterus. This procedure was directly connected to the word "spayed." For us guys it involved making two slits in the sac under our tails large enough for the two testicles to be popped out and removed; this meant we had been "neutered." Bummer! But the bright side of that coin was, Mom would no longer have any more kittens—at her age, a good thing—and my sisters would never know motherhood themselves; probably a good thing too, as they never seemed very responsible to me.

Ten days later we were all returned to the veterinary office for our surgery sites to be rechecked and to receive the remaining distemper combo vaccine as well as the initial feline leukemia shots.

Ouch! I was tired of this; I just wanted to go home. We would all be due back in three weeks for the booster feline leukemia shot. After that, we should be good to go for a whole year, barring any unforeseen disasters.

As soon as we had fully recovered, I asked Mom why we had to endure such indignities. She gathered the four of us together in a partly shaded spot beneath the white oak in our backyard and patiently waited until everyone was comfortably seated. "I have been told that rabies is one of the world's deadliest viruses," she commented, wrapping her paw around my neck to hold me still while she gave my ears a good scrubbing with her tongue. Ugh!

"My grandmother always stressed that almost any warm-blooded mammal could get or carry the rabies virus: foxes, bats, raccoons, coyotes, wolves, dogs—and yes—cats, to name a few. Domesticated pets were the most likely to carry it to unsuspecting humans."

Her voice was raspy with emotion as she continued. "I've heard more recently that other rampant killers have been identified: feline leukemia, FIP, FIV (which is sort of like kitty HIV or AIDS), and feline calicivirus. Some are more deadly than others, yet all are sweeping through unvaccinated cat populations, primarily feral colonies and among outdoor cats or indoor/outdoor cats that are intact and predisposed to fight other cats. Fighting occurs most often during the mating season. Cats that have tested negative for feline leukemia and have been immunized against the disease have a better chance of not acquiring the virus even if they're in contact with cats that test positive.

"Some of the other viruses have no definitive test, no vaccine, and no cure for the disease. Once the disease is contracted, it's only a matter of time before the animal gets sick and dies. It could be weeks or months or years depending on the environment, the animal's diet, and quality of care from onset to demise. The trap-neuter-return (TNR) program, through spaying or neutering, has helped to stem the tide of disease among feral cats somewhat by lessening the urge to fight. TNR also helps by providing food, and, in some fortunate cases, providing donated immunizations, even if they're given just that one time in the cat's life. It may not be perfect, but it's well in front of the alternative."

Mom's voice changed to a stern growl. "As far as you girls go, feral cats should be avoided at all times. They're usually dirty, short tempered, use vile language, are out for food or more likely sex, and have no manners at all! Unless they've found a reliable food source, they're 'here today and gone tomorrow.' So don't be fooled by their sad tales of woe— more than likely it's just a bunch of lies. And you boys stay away from them too, or you'll find yourselves involved in fights you may not win. Remember, ferals may carry disease."

She sighed and then continued. "Now go along, all of you; enough lessons for today."

Her voice had softened and trailed off as she began to take a major bath, even cleaning between her toes. The sun had dipped quite low, and the shadows had lengthened announcing the lateness of the afternoon and, best of all—suppertime!

Chapter 2
Things Happen

NOT LONG AFTER our third trip to the veterinarian's office, some people showed up and took my two sisters away. Mom explained that they had been adopted and had gone to live with another family. Thank goodness; they were always spoiling the fun my brother and I were having, and if we objected they would run and tattle to Mom. She would cuff us behind an ear and tell us to straighten up. We always did what Mom told us to do even if it was for just a short time; then we'd be right back to chasing and tussling, or, our favorite, unrolling the roll of paper in the bathroom. On an especially good day we could make the paper reach all the way to the end of the hall and back. The joys of kittenhood were still upon us. Fun was the name of the game, and we made sure we had fun all day.

Fun is a great thing, but irresponsible fun can be a bad thing. One exceptionally beautiful day our owners had let us out of the house to play in our unfenced yard. After a good tussle on the freshly mown lawn, my brother and I got into a serious game of chase. Round and round the yard we went, under the bushes and through the flower beds. We were so into our game that we became oblivious to all around us. It was then that we committed the ultimate no-no. Down the walkway I streaked, my brother in hot pursuit, but instead of veering right or left at the end, I chose to dash right across the road. I heard the loud squeal of tires behind me, but it was the dull thud that immediately made my blood run cold.

Short of breath, I watched, panting from the opposite side of the street as our owners, alerted by the noise, came running out of the house. By then the car had already stopped and the driver was out of the car, apologizing and stating that he hadn't seen the cats until too late. That small lump in the middle of the road behind the car was my now deceased brother. Oh goodness, I thought, I just killed my brother or caused him to be killed . . . same thing.

I was so upset and scared that I turned around and ran as fast as I could. Terror put blinders on me, and I took no notice of where I was going. I just ran and ran through yards and woods, and down roads totally unfamiliar to me. When exhaustion finally set in, I was miles away from the only home and neighborhood I had ever known. I was lost, really lost. So I hid. I needed rest and to rethink my plight.

The first thing I noticed when I awoke the next morning was how extremely hungry I was. Yesterday's exertions had left me famished. I was also thirsty. I took a quick bath; Mom had always told us to clean up before seeking handouts . . . something about people being more receptive to a clean cat. Then I went about searching for a house. I found one and went to the first door I saw.

"Meow?" I cried. No response. I tried again, "Meow? Meow?" Undaunted I sat down and struck a most appealing pose, not unlike the china cat in the big bay window at home. Ah, home. I made a mental note to retrace my steps just as soon as I got some food. Mom's training reminded me to have patience, but the growl in my belly called for food.

Just then the door flew open and a woman stepped out. "Shoo!" she hissed. "Get on with you. I don't want cats around hunting my birds!"

I was so astounded—never having been spoken to like that before—that I just sat there and stared at her. It was then that I learned what some folks use a broom for. "Scat," she shouted as she whacked me broadside with the broom. It literally knocked me off my feet, out of the trance I was in, and into the bushes.

"Mew." I softened my cry to sound as much like a kitten as I could; I was still in the bushes.

"I said, scat!" she shouted again as she charged, broom held high.

I needed no further convincing and beat a hasty retreat into the woods. Breakfast would not be forthcoming from her.

I wandered through the woods for what seemed like hours, not crossing my trail even once until I came upon another house. Several minutes of meowing and scrambling up onto ledges to peer into the windows revealed that no one was home. Yes, the house was occupied, evidenced by the large, ferocious-looking dog napping in his pen out back, but the owner was away from home, possibly at work. I had no idea what time it was, but with the sun high in the sky, I guessed it was around noon. My stomach attested to it being way past breakfast time. I decided to push on quietly, not wanting to arouse the dog.

I came to a small creek and drank deeply of some much-needed water. It had a bit of grit in it, but I was so hungry and thirsty I didn't care. My thirst temporarily quenched, I gave a quick look around. Nothing seemed to be moving around on the forest floor, but high up in the treetops the squirrels were busily searching for nuts. I gave it a moment's thought before deciding the trees were just too tall and the squirrels too nimble to catch, so I moved on, concentrating on what was at my level on the ground. I had just about given up when I heard a faint rustle in the leaves ahead of me. My whole body instantly went on full alert. All my mom's training came rushing back to me as I crept forward.

As I rounded the base of a hickory tree, a mouse was busily nosing under the leaves for grubs. Every inch of me said this is your chance for breakfast, don't mess it up. One paw at a time I drew closer until I was in perfect position. I stopped, frozen in time except for that darn annoying tip of my tail that always flicked back and forth whenever I tried to be still. I reassessed my distance from the mouse, drew all my muscles together, and pounced. If it hadn't been for the pesky woodpecker that sounded the alarm, I would not have missed. But miss I did and no amount of grabbing at leaves where the mouse should have been produced a mouse. Oh spit, spit, spiffel! I was really hungry now.

Again I looked around; the forest behind me was dark and dank, but the area ahead and to the right appeared brighter than where I'd been, so I decided to go that way. Before long, sunlight was bespeckling the forest floor. Maybe I had finally made a good choice.

As I reached the clearing and stepped out into the full sunlight there were houses up and down the street; some had white picket fences, some no fences at all, but all had well-manicured lawns. Nice, relatively new cars were parked in each driveway; no rattle traps here, and there was a feeling of welcome coming from all directions. For the first time in nearly twenty-four hours I didn't feel lost or afraid. Tail held high to show confidence, I sauntered up the street toward an area where the pavement spread out into a big circle. I needed to have a look-see before I committed myself.

As I approached the cul-de-sac, I noticed a woman sitting on a walkway planting flowers. I ducked under an azalea bush and watched her intently. She looked very relaxed and seemed quite happy at her work. I didn't see a broom anywhere near her. Hunger pains were gnawing at me again. Just as I was about to introduce myself to her, I stopped dead in my tracks. Who or what was that walking towards her? It walked like a cat, meowed like a cat, even looked like a cat in a floor-length fur coat, but I'd never seen anything like it before; all my family had been shorthaired.

The cat, rubbing her body down the woman's thigh, showed great affection for the lady. From what I could see of the lavish attention she was receiving in return, the feeling seemed to be mutual. Her coat was long and silky, and it was evident from her curviness that she rarely missed a meal. Her emerald green eyes augmented the gold, copper, and silver swirls in her tortoiseshell coloring. She was a dish to look at.

Dish! The very thought sent new pangs of hunger throughout my body. By now I was sure I was going to starve to death. Maybe, just maybe, this lady would prepare something for me to eat. I snuck slowly out from under the bush. The cat was the first to see me, and she alerted the lady with all manner of hisses, spits, and growls. I was in full retreat back to the azalea bush when the lady said, "Fuzzbucket, everything will be OK." Then she called out ever so softly to me, "Here, kitty, kitty. Here, kitty. Are you hungry? Just wait; I'll get you something to eat."

She scooped Fuzzbucket up into her arms and dashed inside the house. Why I chose to stay with a cat like Fuzzbucket around, I honestly don't know. After all, I would be crossing into her territory.

In no time the lady returned with a plate full of wet food and a bowl of clear, cool, clean water. She placed them on the porch and stepped back. "Here, kitty, kitty. Come get a bite to eat," she invited. I simply could not help myself; the aroma was too enticing. Throwing all caution to the wind, I calmly walked up to the plate, sat down, and ate. It was heavenly.

Fuzzbucket

Chapter 3
First Things First

FUZZBUCKET, SAFELY INSIDE the house, was beside herself. "Usurper! Rogue! Beggar!" she screamed at me through the plate glass picture window above me. With her paws pressed tightly against the window and tail furiously lashing back and forth, she added several more unladylike insults to her rant. Any other time I might have taken offense at the expletives she hurled at me, but I was so intent on satisfying my intense hunger that I plain didn't care. I had had a plate of food given solely to me. I didn't have to share it, and I intended to savor each bite to the utmost, regardless of how anyone else felt about it. I simply got up, walked around to the other side of the plate, and with my back to the window sat down and continued to eat.

The gesture, subtle as it was, was not wasted on the lady. She coughed slightly to cover a snicker. Fuzzbucket, on the other hand, continued hurling whatever insults came to mind. Mom would have been proud of the way I let them roll off me like water droplets. It seemed I had grown up a lot in the last twenty-four hours.

Having eaten as much as my now taut belly would hold, I stood up, walked straight over to my benefactress, and rubbed the whole length of my body against her leg; after all, she deserved a lot of thanks, and I planned to give it my best. She reached down and rubbed her hand gently along my back. As good as the touch felt, I still felt a need to be wary, so I slid out from under her hand and moved a few feet away. I could see she was watching me, so I sat down and took the most bodacious bath I could muster. That should convince her I appreciated all she had done for me.

She walked over and picked up the empty plate but left the bowl of water. "This is for later in case you get thirsty during the night," she said. "I'll expect you bright and early in the morning for breakfast, so if I were you I'd find a place to your liking somewhere close. You should be quite safe." She tossed the words over her shoulder as she disappeared into the house.

"You bet I will," I purred in reply.

It was getting dark, so I sniffed around for a snug place to spend the night. I had to hurry as the neighborhood was new to me. I checked the basement, but the door was closed. The old garage was so dark inside that I decided to wait until morning to venture in. And then, there was the obvious—a padded swing and two padded rocking chairs on the porch. They were positioned to provide an excellent view of the front yard and cul-de-sac. Best of all, the side and back of the porch were so high off the ground that nothing but a lizard could scale the brick walls. I hopped up on the cushioned swing. It felt so soft and I was so exhausted I could go no farther. I snuggled down among the extra pillows, curled up, and fell fast asleep.

Dawn arrived and I was rested and ready to face the day. I climbed out of the pillows, jumped lightly down from the swing, stretched my longest stretch including all eighteen toes, yawned my widest yawn, and went to get a drink of water from the dish; this water was a vast improvement over the sandy creek water.

After another quick body check, I removed a piece of lint from my paw and gave several good licks to smooth the white hair on my chest. Now I felt ready for whatever the day might bring. I waited, but nothing happened. I jumped up to the picture window ledge and peered in—nothing. I paced back and forth in front of the door where I had last seen the lady, and I called with the most piteous meows, but nothing was going on, not even a rustle. My hunger was beginning to rise. "Oh, woe is me. She promised breakfast bright and early."

I waited another fifteen minutes or so before I decided to try my luck down the street. From the look of things where I was, it might be worth my while. When I passed by yesterday, I had made a mental note that the house with the white picket fence and lots of flower gardens showed promise. The homeowners there really cared about their property. Just as I was preparing to squeeze through the pickets in the fence, I heard the sound I had been waiting for. "Here, kitty, kitty. Here, kitty, kitty. Breakfast," the lady called from up the street.

"Meow, meow, meow," I answered as I raced back to her front porch. "I'm coming; I'm coming; please don't go away and take my breakfast with you. I never meant to leave, I promise," I meowed. I couldn't see anything wrong with a little white lie when breakfast was at stake.

"Well, it's about time you showed up. Where did you go so early this morning?" she asked. "You almost missed breakfast."

"Oh no," I meowed. "Not that!"

"You certainly are a talker, aren't you? Here you're pleading your case just like a politician," she muttered as a smile spread across her face. "You need to have a more fitting name than Kitty, and the most talkative politicians I know of are senators when they're filibustering. Senator seems to fit you, so Senator it is. Do you like the name Senator?" she asked, just like I was a person.

"Meow," I answered. I didn't have the foggiest notion what the lady was talking about, but I was delighted to see the plate of wet food accompanied by a bowl of dry crunchy bits and another bowl of fresh, cool water; no slacker here. Now, what was that name I was supposed to answer to? Oh yes, Senator. Well, if it was OK with her, it was OK with me. I even thought it sounded a bit distinguished. And yes, breakfast was indeed delicious.

Chapter 4
Fuzzbucket

FUZZBUCKET DISDAINED TO rush to the food dish; she preferred to be fashionably late, so it became her habit to stay snuggled up in the bed sheets and down comforter after her mistress had risen and dressed for the morning. She knew her owner would return to change for work after lunch and would make up the bed at that time, which would be long after Fuzzbucket had vacated it in search of food and a litter box. Her mistress worked the second shift, 3:00 to 11:00 p.m. Missing work for snow days was not an option, so her schedule rarely changed. All the cats in the household knew her schedule by rote and reveled in the extra attention they received on her days off. It was a good, reliable life for all.

It goes without saying that Fuzzbucket ruled the roost with iron claws. Small of stature and tough as nails, she was a formidable adversary when crossed. Every cat in the household knew this, and everyone complied. Even the larger, younger Toms gave her plenty of space when she was in one of her moods. All the cats in the lady's care had been spayed or neutered, so the term "Tom" was used loosely to designate any male, despite being neutered.

Fuzzbucket had just finished breakfast and was making her usual rounds when she remembered her unfinished business with the usurper from the night before. "How could I have forgotten such an important state of affairs," she grumbled to herself as she dashed to the picture window. Her worst fears were realized: there I was, eating, without as much as a by-your-leave, on her porch; the audacity of it all.

Tensing every muscle, she let out a tremendous yowl. It should have put everyone on notice that she was thoroughly provoked, but when she looked out the window again, I was still there, eating the last morsels of my breakfast. I did flick an ear in her direction as if to say, "Where I come from, ladies do not use that kind of language. What's your problem?"

"How dare you ignore my warning like that; no one else does. I'll scratch your nose when I get a chance," she spat through the glass.

"What on earth for? I haven't done anything to deserve that," I stated as I left the now-empty bowls and approached the window. On the inside, Fuzzbucket's instant fury caused every hair on her body to stick out, making her seem twice her normal size.

"Stay back," she hissed as her ears flattened against her head. "I'll scratch. I swear I will."

"Suit yourself," I replied. "I'm not from these parts and was just hoping that a beautiful cat such as you might be able to tell me about this neighborhood."

There was a very long pause on her part. I could see the wheels turning in her head as she thought it over. "Why, I guess I could show you around a bit," she said. Apparently, no one had ever been so suave with her before. She must have been impressed at how handsome I was for a stray, not a hair out of place; my black and white coat just shone with health, and I walked with confidence. Suddenly her demeanor changed; she calmed down.

"I would like to meet you too," she purred. The other cats in the house, who had gathered at the first yowl, sat down and watched Fuzzbucket; they seemed amazed. They must not have ever seen her so docile, and they weren't about to change her mood.

For several days Fuzzbucket and I continued to get to know each other through the picture window. Breakfast and supper drew me back to the porch at the appointed times. I made sure I was there well-washed, slicked down. I was determined that no one would beat me out of my tasty vittles. I think it was because of my promptness and docile, well-mannered attitude that the lady of the house took extra time to pat and talk to me, which I didn't mind at all. I reciprocated by rubbing against her, bumping her hand with my head, and making a soft, peculiar noise in my throat.

I don't remember if I had purred since I was a very young kitten. At that time it was a sort of self-satisfied soft rumble that occurred when I kneaded Mom's warm belly with my front paws as I nursed. It gave me an exquisite feeling of bliss, tranquility, and contentment. I guess it came back because I began to have those feelings again. It seemed to please the lady very much, so I practiced my rediscovered purr at every opportunity. Things had indeed turned out well.

The most important thing to me was that I had decided to accept my new name: Senator. Regardless of whether I was pursuing a fascinating bug hunt or exploring a new section of the yard when I heard my name called, I came.

The day finally arrived when I got the opportunity to meet Fuzzbucket nose to nose. One would have thought she had never laid eyes on me by the way she jumped back and hissed. To be honest, I believe it was just a ploy for her to reestablish her dominance. I didn't even give it another thought. She was the way she wanted to be, and I would continue to be my calm, diplomatic, handsome self. Actually, I was shaking in my boots, so to speak. It was not that long ago that she had hissed some pretty awful things at me. No, I hadn't forgotten.

"Come on now," I purred. "You promised to show me around and be my friend."

"I'll show you around when I please," she spat back. "I'm the top cat around here and you'd better not forget it. I never promised to be your friend; you'll have to earn that." She turned around and marched off at a leisurely pace, head high and tail held up with a slight bend at the tip. In all her haughtiness she was still a magnificent creature.

Fuzzbucket

Chapter 5
Gabby

THE NEXT DAY I set off down the road. I needed to know what other cats lived on the street. Fuzzbucket didn't seem interested, so I went on my own. I passed the house next door and the one with the white picket fence across the street without incident. I was making good time as I passed the empty lot with a chain link fence when my attention was drawn to a yellow cat sitting in the middle of the road.

"And just who might you be?" she hissed as she blocked my way.

"I'm called Senator, and I'm learning my new neighborhood. Do you know anything about it?"

"Of course I do, I live here; Miss G and her husband, Harry, live over there behind the picket fence; the folks next door have five children; but I shouldn't be talking to you, I don't know anything about you."

"What do you want to know?" I sensed the aura of knowledge about her, and I felt I could trust her.

"Since I've never seen you around before, you must be a stray. Where did you come from? Are you carrying any diseases? Have you been vaccinated?" She yawned as if totally bored with our conversation.

I assured her that I had been neutered and had my shots. I was still out of sorts about the rabies vaccination. Apparently, I let my feelings show because she invited me to join her in the shade on her lawn.

"They call me Gabby because I like to tell what I know. You are still very young. Maybe I can help you understand why some unpleasant things are so necessary.

"Many years ago when I was just a teenage kitten, and my young owner was taking pre-veterinary courses, she'd read aloud essays that she had written to sound them out. I loved the sweet sound of her voice, so I'd listen carefully; I didn't just lick the knowledge of such things up off the grass, you know. They involved many subjects, but the one I remember most vividly—because it was so scary—was about viruses, and in particular the consequences of contracting the rabies virus.

"Long, long ago before rabies vaccines were invented, people who came in contact with or were bitten by a rabid animal died! If infected, humans could pass it on to other humans through their saliva—either before or soon after death. Those humans would 'go mad,' foaming at the mouth and running around in a crazed manner. This particular symptom gave rise during the Middle and Dark Ages to a belief in werewolves. Since there was no cure and no vaccine to ward it off, the only means of control was to kill the infected animal."

She paused momentarily to see if I was listening and to check the yard for lurking dangers. Satisfied that all was in order, she continued. "Life wasn't easy back then. If I remember correctly, in 1885, or near that time, Louis Pasteur invented a vaccine that prevented the rabies virus from infecting an animal exposed to the disease. Sadly, this wasn't necessarily done to save the animal; it was to protect any human that had had contact with an infected animal and might be at risk. The only surefire test we have, even now, to determine whether an animal carries the rabies virus, is to kill it and study its brain tissue; it's the only way to be absolutely sure. Therefore, if a human is bitten and the animal escapes and isn't found, the only option is for the person to undergo a series of four rabies shots, the first to be given as soon as possible after the bite. They may also require a fifth shot; a dose of rabies immune globulin, followed by rabies shots on the third, seventh, and fourteenth day. I've been told that it works in most cases if treated soon enough.

"Animals that have been exposed to another animal with rabies aren't always so lucky. Only if they've received rabies vaccinations regularly—their owners must have proof of current vaccinations and be willing to quarantine their pet for ten or more days in an approved place—are they even allowed to live. Those that aren't current on the vaccine, even by one or two days, are usually required to be euthanized and their brain tissue tested, even if they didn't bite anyone. It's a sad state of affairs and not one to be taken lightly." Lowering her eyes, she coughed and shook her head slightly. If cats could cry, I would have sworn she shed a tear.

"Gabby,"—I was almost afraid to ask—"what happened to the young girl that owned you back then? Why aren't you with her?"

"She was killed in a car accident her first year in veterinary school. It was very early and we were on the way to the school; she'd made an appointment for me to be spayed that morning, and she was scheduled to assist; it would be a first for both of us. A man in too much of a hurry ran a red light and wrapped our car around the front of his vehicle.

"As long as I'd been with her, she'd never seen any reason to confine me to a carrier when we went out for rides in her car; I just lay beside her thigh on the front seat. She provided a non-breakaway collar that I always wore, and when we would get out of the car, I walked on a leash right beside her. The minute the car stopped sliding, I jumped across her limp body and out through the broken driver's side window. I knew she was dead; animals, cats in particular, have a sixth sense about such things.

"My landing on the pavement must have been hard; I was found several days later, hungry and scared, limping around an unfamiliar neighborhood. Unfortunately, I had fractured my left front leg directly across the growth plate. My rescuers knew I wasn't feral by the collar I was wearing, but they had no idea who I belonged to. Without someone to pay for the surgery to set the leg, the tech simply bandaged it and gave me to a family who promised to take care of me. When I became pregnant the first time, it was decided they couldn't keep me and gave me away. The owners I have now were the ones willing to take me, even though I was in a family way. I've been with them ever since. Many years have passed since then."

The long shadows, indicating the lateness of the afternoon, brought me to my feet. My stomach growled, so I apologized for staying so late. It was time to eat.

"Oh alright, come with me. I have my own entrance," Gabby said as she limped toward the rear of the house. We entered through a cat flap door into the mud room just off the kitchen. A fresh bowl of water and a bowl of dry food were on a mat to the right of the door. I sat down and gave my face a good wash while Gabby ate first. When she moved away, I went over and finished what she had left.

The lady of the house entered the kitchen and spied us. "Who have you brought in this time, Gabby? I can't keep up with all your friends, let alone feed them. Now get back outside, both of you, while I clean up."

The broom incident of several days ago still fresh in my memory, I beat a hasty retreat out the cat door; Gabby climbed awkwardly through behind me.

"Don't be alarmed; she won't hurt you. I hope you'll come join me for supper again." Never known to have turned down an offer of a free meal, I returned often. My eager attendance prompted Gabby's owners to install an electronic cat flap with a special collar for Gabby that unlocked it when she needed to enter. It barred the entrance of any animal not wearing one; me, in particular.

Gabby was never as friendly after that; I got the distinct feeling she blamed me for having to wear the electronic collar. So I only visited occasionally and never tried to re-enter her house. Our talks on the lawn became fewer too.

As she aged, she became increasingly intolerant of affection even from her owners. Her limp was more apparent, and it seemed to bother her more. Eventually, old injuries brought on unmanageable pain and her veterinarian came to the house and mercifully put her to sleep.

I do miss the informative chats we had.

Chapter 6
For Whom the Bells Toll

As THE YEARS PASSED Fuzzbucket and I did become close friends, although I never lived in the house with her. I preferred the freedom of being outdoors, but we socialized a lot when she was allowed outside. She was many years my senior and I learned a lot from her, even if it was what not to do. For whatever reason, some cats don't spend as much time grooming as others, especially as they age. This quirk can lead to a buildup of unshed undercoat that over time forms mats and are the dickens to get rid of. They usually require a vigorous combing or clipping to remove them. If scissors are used, the groomer must be very careful not to cut the skin, as mats often will be tightly formed close to the body.

Fuzzbucket was beginning to lose interest in grooming, but our lady kept right on it and continued to comb and brush her often. She kept a pin brush on the table right beside her recliner for just such occasions. Although Fuzzbucket fussed and wiggled at first, she'd eventually settle into our lady's lap and allow the grooming to take place. If the truth be known, I think she basked in all the attention.

It seems to me that both long- and short-haired cats living in an air-conditioned environment do not shed their undercoats as they should and are more prone to form mats than cats that spend some of the day outside in the heat. However, the cats that do go outside will sometimes pick up sticks, leaves, seeds, or burrs that stick in their coats or tail hairs, causing mats to form. Good health is in the eye of the beholder, so it is up to the caregivers to check for mats often and remove them ASAP.

If cats that groom attempt to remove a mat from their fur it can make them prone to getting hairballs. Our rough tongues act to smooth our coats and remove any loose hair, which is almost always swallowed due to the way the tongue's barbs point backward toward the throat. If lucky, we'll "cough up" the swallowed hair, usually in the form of a cylindrical mass, accompanied by some stomach fluids and contents. Although our caregivers may not be keen on this happening and may hate having to clean it up, it is possible for far worse problems to occur. If the hairball remains in the stomach or intestines too long, it may collect enough hair to cause a blockage, which would require manual manipulation or surgery to remove. It can become a really big deal.

Less than five years after I had first met her, Fuzzbucket's roaming days were over. She went into the house at night but insisted on being outside during the day, despite having lost most of her hearing ability. She slept for hours in the sun-warmed shade under the bushes that surrounded the front yard. Sometimes she curled up in a patch of long grass our lady had left to make a soft bed for her. This grassy spot was the last place anyone saw her.

We think a coyote came into the yard from the woods and found her asleep. It's likely that she didn't hear the creature approach and it easily took her away. I can only hope he was quick and merciful. Coyotes are relentless hunters and are known to prey on small mammals, including small dogs and cats.

A few weeks later there was news of a woman that lived several streets away who was attacked by a coyote. As she was working in her yard along with her gardener, she suffered numerous bites on her face and arms before the gardener was able to kill the beast with a shovel. The gardener also suffered bites on his hands and legs. Both were rushed to the hospital where their wounds were treated. Because of the strange behavior and unprovoked aggression of the coyote, both of them had to undergo the series of four rabies prevention shots in addition to a dose of rabies immune globulin. Tests later proved that the coyote was rabid. Having heard this news, we all became aware that coyotes were invading our residential neighborhood. Everyone continues to remain on high alert. Fortunately, to the best of my knowledge, no more coyotes have been seen in our vicinity.

But I am way ahead of my story.

Chapter 7
Masked Marauders

I SPENT THE rest of that summer basking in the sun and cooling in the shade. Having been introduced to Wendell, Wendy, and Rascal, the other cats in the house, there was plenty of companionship. I did occasionally wonder how Mom was doing, having lost all her family in such a short time, but as the years wore on, I thought less and less about it.

I definitely had learned to live in the here and now, and I spent many hours with the triplets Wendell, Wendy, and Rascal. All of them had been rescued from a dumpster by the railroad tracks. They were orange tabbies and from all indications from the same litter. Their mom was too feral to capture, too wily to trap.

Our lady had fallen completely in love with their antics and didn't have the heart to put them up for adoption. She took them to the vet's office for kitten wellness checkups and their shots, as well as for spaying and neutering. Wendell was found to have a severe case of ear mites that the tech treated with a drop or two of medicine in each ear. Our lady was given a small bottle to take home for further treatments.

Ear infections can move inward to the middle ear; in some cases, the cat scratching and shaking its head can cause a hematoma (blood clot) in the outer ear or even a ruptured eardrum. Cats with severe ear infections may hold their head to one side. Loss of balance or walking in circles may be signs of a deep infection. Surgery may be required to clean the ear, but with no guarantee that the cat will regain its equilibrium. An ounce of prevention—by paying close attention to ear cleanliness—really is worth more than the money spent to try to cure it.

Once treated, the triplets were put back into the carrier and into the car for the trip home. Not a peep was heard out of them as they snuggled together for solace and warmth. Since then, they have all lived together in a very special house.

Our lady had cat flap doors installed in the front door as well as the door to the large unfurnished basement and the basement door to the outside so that we could enter and exit at will. She could lock the entry flap on each with a metal slide if needed, to secure the house.

It was a nifty arrangement: I was fed on the porch, and the others ate indoors in the kitchen. We all knew the rules and followed them to the letter. It was perfect until the gang of sharp-nosed, beady-eyed bandits showed up, intent on stealing my food. The bandits were raccoons. There were big males, smaller females, and little ones, all looking for a handout. Our lady was enthralled with them; the little ones wanted to play with her toes if she was barefooted. She supplied dry dog food as treats. Personally, I was not impressed. They'd usurped my territory and made eating in peace impossible. The larger males soon became quite aggressive and wouldn't let me eat at all. It was my first experience with a gaze (group) of raccoons and I didn't like it. Having been warned by my mom about raccoons carrying rabies, I certainly didn't want a fight, so I left. I marched down to the house with the white picket fence, intent on moving there.

I'd already introduced myself to the elderly couple that owned the house during one of my earlier explorations of the area and had learned their names from Gabby. The husband, Harry, liked to take walks around the neighborhood. His wife, Miss G, was most pleasant and enjoyed being out in the yard tending her flowers. I loved the companionship and spent many hours sitting with her as she gardened. It didn't take much of an invitation to convince me to move in.

I continued to check daily on my other home. On the days she was working, our lady left the house around two in the afternoon and didn't return until after eleven at night. It should have been the perfect arrangement it had been previously, but the marauding masked bandits weren't content with what she provided for them before she left.

One evening while she was at work and I was at her house checking on things, two of the gang discovered the cat door; before anyone could stop them, in they went. Curiosity had got the better of them, and their keen sense of smell led them straight to the kitchen. I had followed at a safe distance and was appalled at what happened next. They trashed everything, knocking things off counters onto the floor in their search for food. And when they did find it, they ripped the bags of dry food to pieces. Of course, a fight for the best food ensued, adding to the mess. Their hunger finally sated, they left the way they came, leaving total disarray behind them.

When our lady returned, she was flabbergasted to find such a mess. I was still in the house, afraid to leave. At first she thought that maybe the triplets and I had gotten into a squabble. But soon she realized it had to have been something else. As if on cue, she turned around to face one of the perpetrators, who had returned for more goodies.

"Oh no! How'd you get in here?" she asked as she chased it through the dining room and into the living room. She was close enough almost to catch it as it beat a hasty retreat through the cat door. "Aha!" Her jubilance at solving the mystery of access was quickly squashed by reality. "Drat, now I'll have to keep the cat doors closed and locked all the time," she said with a sigh. "The kitties will not like this one bit. Darn those 'coons anyway."

I could have told her there would be a problem; the number of raccoons showing up for food had skyrocketed in the last few days. I hoped she would do something about them and soon. My daily routine had been upended and I didn't appreciate it one bit.

The very next day she made a call to the county animal control, and they referred her to a wild animal control service. The person answering at the Critter Ridder Services informed her politely that some raccoons harbor the rabies virus for up to seven or more months before showing any signs of the disease; therefore, all raccoons were considered carriers of the deadly virus and couldn't be relocated. The long and short of it was that any raccoons they trapped would be euthanized according to state law. There were no exceptions.

It was indeed a bitter pill for a staunch animal lover like our lady to swallow. On the other hand, she needed to rid herself of the potential threat to herself and her cats. I'm proud to report that she included me as one of her cats. I was once again "owned," and, it felt great. To celebrate the accomplishment, I sat down and took another bodacious bath, paying close attention to the backs of my ears, the tip of my tail, and the white spots on my chest. Oh joy, oh joy, I now belonged to her.

She continued her inquiry. "How soon can you start trapping? What's the cost and how often do you check the traps to see if you've been successful?"

The reply was short but not too sweet. "Next Monday we can come in the late afternoon and set and bait humane traps in your yard. We'll be back early the next morning to check them, remove any animals caught, then re-bait and reset the traps. We'll continue this daily until we've trapped as many animals as you want to be removed. Your cost will be one hundred and twenty-five dollars per raccoon we remove."

"One hundred and twenty-five dollars per 'coon?" She gasped. "What if you catch a possum by mistake? What happens then?"

"Possums are half price if you want them removed. Otherwise, we just release them back onto your property. They're not rabies carriers and don't have to be destroyed." The answer was very concise.

Zowie, that sounded like a lot of money to me! I couldn't understand why she didn't just thank the man and hang up. She could probably find someone to move them into the mountains and release them; no one would know. "At least they would have a chance to live," I muttered to myself. I felt horrible that I'd been so quick to have them gone.

"I must warn you that to catch a raccoon and take it to another site and release it is not an option," said the man on the line. "To do so and get caught carries a twenty-five thousand dollar fine, so we won't even entertain the notion; I don't recommend that you do either."

That man on the phone must have read my mind, I thought, as I jumped up onto the picture window sill to gain a safer advantage. My move was purely a gut reaction and had nothing to do with my being in immediate danger.

"You said possums are half price? Does that mean I have to pay sixty-two fifty for each possum you trap?" she asked.

"Only if we remove them from your property; for the ones we catch and release there's no charge."

"Well, that's a relief. Can we keep my cats out of the traps?" It was a question I was glad she'd asked.

"Usually, cats don't enter our traps. We bait them with marshmallows—not usually a cat attractant. However, we do catch an extraordinarily curious cat from time to time. Cats are pretty vocal about being caught and the homeowner will usually hear them. We'll instruct you on how to release the cat without harm, or we can release it each morning. An overnight stay typically won't harm a cat, but most of our cat owner clients prefer to release them as soon as possible, even if it's the middle of the night. It'd be up to you," the man said.

"I see." She sighed. I could tell she was upset and worried. "Do you give quantity discounts?"

"It depends. I'd have to ask my boss. How many raccoons are we talking about?"

"That's the problem. I don't know. Maybe sixteen to twenty, but there could be more. The critters just keep showing up. I can't tell which ones have been here before or which ones are new. I just don't know if I can afford to remove them all right now."

"I can just about guarantee you that not removing most or all of them will just attract more. Raccoons are territorial and tend to move in circles. They'll leave for a while, but nine times out of ten they'll come back to recheck their foraging area." It was the phone person's way of telling her it would indeed be expensive. "I'll ask my boss about a discount. I know he'll try to help you any way he can."

She gave him a phone number where she could be reached. He promised to get back to her as soon as he could. She thanked him, hung up the phone, and wept.

I felt so sorry for her that I hopped down, crossed the living room, crawled right up beside her in her overstuffed recliner, and we snuggled together. I'd never before allowed myself to be caught up so completely in an emotional moment. It was sort of scary at first, and because I didn't know what to do exactly, I sat as still as I could. Her light touch patting my head and stroking my body did its magic and soon I was purring quite happily. She seemed to relax too.

The friends our lady consulted seemed of one opinion: she had no other choice than to rid herself of the inherent dangers of a large raccoon population.

"What if one of the 'coons got into the house during the night and attacked you while you were sleeping?" asked a neighbor.

"Aren't you concerned about exposing your cats?" asked another.

"That's an awful lot of money!" was the response most often heard.

"No kidding," was our lady's disheartened reply. "Tell me something I don't know!"

As soon as she had the time she went to her financial advisor at the bank. After some fancy figuring and careful transfer of funds from one account to another, her advisor was able to free up enough cash to swing the deal.

"I moved enough money to your checking account to cover a small additional amount should you need it. Don't worry; you have enough to pay to have all the raccoons removed. Now just do it." Her advisor patted her on the shoulder as she escorted her to the door. "Don't worry; everything will be all right."

Our lady nodded and left the bank. Tears of gratitude and sorrow welled up in her eyes as she slipped behind the wheel. "Oh, oh, all my little bandits…" She made a call on her cell phone. "Come and set your traps Monday," was all she could manage to say before she hung up.

The Critter Ridders arrived Monday as promised. They offered a 10 percent reduction in price if they caught and removed sixteen or more. All told, they trapped and removed twenty-two raccoons by the end of the second week. No more raccoons showed up to be caught. We cats all breathed a sigh of relief. Our lady, though very stressed during the ordeal, seemed a lot more at ease and relaxed when all was said and done.

The three possums that were caught during the process were released back into the woods behind the house. Two of them still appear almost nightly for a quick snack! The third one visited for several months before disappearing. We haven't seen him since.

Chapter 8
A New Name

WENDY, RASCAL, AND Wendell have all passed on, crossed over the Rainbow Bridge. They're buried in our kitty cemetery near the woods behind the house. It's ivy-covered, shady, and serene. There's a bench for anyone who wants to pause and visit. Headstones with every cat's name and date deceased mark each grave. Statues of St. Francis and several angels watch over them. It's so beautiful and quiet; it's where I want to be placed when I'm gone.

After the raccoons had been removed and it was safe for us cats to be out and about again—well, as safe as can be expected for outdoor cats—I decided to revisit the folks in the house behind the white picket fence.

Miss G and Harry were delighted to have me back and invited me in. They plied me with all sorts of yummy treats until I could eat no more. To show my appreciation, I got up on the arm of the chair where Miss G was sitting and let her rub my head and stroke my body. I'd learned that this gesture gave our lady lots of pleasure; I could see no reason for it not to work with Miss G too. To add to the enjoyment of the moment, I purred and purred and purred.

"Looks like you have a new friend," her husband said.

"Not so new; he gardened with me almost all summer, but this is the first time he's been in our house. I think he belongs to Maggie up the street. He always comes from that direction," said Miss G as she smiled and stroked my fur.

My ears pricked up and I opened one eye. "Maggie. So that's our lady's name, Maggie. Sounds OK to me," I thought just before I fell asleep.

The couple chatted on and on, obviously enjoying each other's company. I might've caught a word or two here and there, but I mostly dozed. It wasn't until Miss G got up, apologizing that she had to disturb me, that I became fully awake. Miss G was on the way to the kitchen to fix their dinner when it struck me how very late it was. I was sorely disappointed I'd missed supper at our lady's ... er ... Maggie's house. Completely flustered, I ran to the front door meowing loudly.

"Looks like our guest wants out again," Harry called to his wife in the kitchen.

"Oh, alright, but not until I feed him. It's late and Maggie may have already fed the other cats." Two meows from me and she appeared with a plate of deboned boiled chicken, which she put down right where I was at the front door. I simply couldn't get it eaten fast enough. I had so thoroughly convinced myself that I had already missed my dinner at Maggie's that I even forgot my pre-dinner bath. I worked doubly hard to clean myself once the plate was removed.

Moments later the phone rang. It was Maggie asking if they'd seen me. She was worried when I didn't show up for supper. If there was one thing definite about me, it was that you could call me anything, but don't call me late for dinner! Miss G assured her I was with them and had just finished supper. Maggie thanked her, advised her that I needed to use the outdoors rather than a litter box, and hung up.

"I just learned our guest has a name. Maggie says she calls him Senator because of his talkative nature," Miss G told Harry.

Miss G let me out as they were on the way to bed. She felt sure I knew how to take care of myself; after all, I'd been staying out at Maggie's. Thanks to the sound advice and training I got from my mom, I was prepared.

From that day forward I spent most of my time with Miss G in the garden or with her in her favorite chair. But I never forgot what a wonderful home Maggie had provided, and on days Miss G was not available, I sauntered up the street to visit my old haunt. Maggie was always delighted to see me and made me feel right at home as if I'd never left.

It was this quirk of mine that prompted Harry to rename me Senator Bollweevil; as he saw it, I was always looking for a home. The name stuck and even today, although I am in my golden years as an indoor-only cat, I'm still known by that moniker. I don't mind; I think it rather fits me.

Chapter 9
A Stranger in Our Midst

A CAT MAGGIE named Stranger was the first blue point Siamese Maggie or I had ever seen, not that I ever believed he was a purebred. His coat was so dirty and scraggly Maggie couldn't tell what color he was when he first arrived. Both of his eyes were matted and drained fluid from the inside corners, and his tail was full of tiny grass burrs. He was skinny as a rake and walked gingerly on his obviously sore foot pads. To say he was a mess was the understatement of the day.

Maggie immediately recognized a cat in great need and ran into the house for a plate of food. But he shied away the minute she returned, and no amount of coaxing could persuade him to come and eat. Finally, she set the plate down on the porch and called me into the house.

"Come on, Senator," she whispered. "Let's go in and let this stranger eat. We can watch from the window."

I trotted right in, hoping some of the food left would be for me, but we didn't head for the kitchen. Instead, Maggie went to the window and stared out. I hopped up on the sill right beside her. The strange cat was still standing on the walk where he'd been when we went inside. He had made no effort to approach the plate, much less eat. I must've shown some of my frustration because Maggie reached over and stroked my fur.

"We must be patient and not hurry him," she said. "He needs time to sort things out and learn to trust again."

She said she'd received an e-mail a week ago about a lost Siamese cat in our community. It said the owners were moving and that when the moving van came to pick up their furniture, the cat bolted out the door and ran away. The owners tried to find it, but in the short time before they left they didn't succeed. They contacted the person who sends news items to residents of our community and asked to be alerted if anyone should find their cat. And then they left; they had no choice. From the look of things, no one had gotten close enough to see him let alone report him found. Maggie told me she was pretty sure this was that cat.

We remained there watching him out the window, and he stayed right where he was, watching us. Finally, Maggie realized that she needed to be doing other things and we moved away from the window. It was early in the day, and Miss G had gone to her weekly hair appointment, so I was in no hurry to leave. I just curled up in Maggie's overstuffed recliner and napped. In my dreams I recalled the uncertainty I felt in leaving my first home; I definitely could empathize with the strange cat on the walkway.

When Maggie came back to the living room, I woke up and looked out the window with her. Both the cat and the food were gone.

"See, I told you," Maggie said with a big smile on her face. "He just needed his privacy."

The next morning he was back, at a safe distance, but the food she put out for him disappeared quickly. Each morning repeated itself until you could see a definite improvement in his demeanor. One day he surprised all of us and sat down on the walk and took a bath. Whoever said you have to feel good about yourself before you can improve your appearance certainly knew what they were talking about.

Somewhere around this same time, the Siamese began to take an interest in what Maggie was doing. You could see his desire for attention; he watched her like a hawk. He wanted to go up to Maggie; you could tell he wanted to and tried to make himself approach her, but in the end he just couldn't do it. He'd go off to the corner of the yard, sit down, and continue to stare at her.

Maggie could feel his hesitancy, but she couldn't figure a way to solve the problem. She believed that she could teach him to trust her if only she could get her hands on him. She knew that he needed to go to the vet for a thorough checkup and treatment. She was worried about her own cats, not knowing anything about his status with vaccinations, especially the rabies vaccine. She'd tried to contact the former owners shortly after he arrived, but the address they'd left at the community hotline was apparently not correct, so after several attempts she gave up. This strange cat was now hers to take care of.

In desperation, Maggie phoned her childhood friend Draya to see if she knew how to catch the cat; she told her how timid it was. Draya asked if she had a medium-sized plastic pet carrier. The answer being yes, Draya suggested that she place the carrier on the porch and put his plate of food inside.

"Do this every feeding for several days," Draya said. "Then, when he gets used to going into the carrier to be fed, sit down beside the carrier and be very still. When he enters the carrier to eat, quickly close the door and latch it tightly; then take him right to the vet's office. Remember, you think he was once an indoor kitty and was probably used to being handled. We just don't know if he was handled with TLC or roughly. But I guess we'll find out, won't we?"

It took about a week, but the ploy worked and off he went to the vet. When Maggie filled out the initial paperwork to add him to her account, she realized he had to have a name. Without hesitation she wrote Stranger; that was what she'd called him in her mind all along.

Stranger endured the initial vet check with incredible poise and dignity. He got all his vaccines in one fell swoop. The veterinarian told Maggie that it was possible he might not feel too well when he got home, but he should be okay the next day.

As to the weeping eyes, the doctor determined that his tear ducts hadn't properly formed. The tubes that normally drained the lubricating fluid from his eyes out through his nose were nonexistent, and any extra fluid produced would just spill over at the corners of his eyes. "I don't think it can be easily repaired," the vet said. "He'll just have to live with it for the rest of his life."

He told Maggie that if his eyes got too crusty, she could wipe them with a tissue. He'd be okay. He'd already been neutered so she didn't have that to worry about that. After the flea treatment was applied, Maggie paid the bill and brought Stranger home.

The change in Stranger was amazing. From the minute he was released from the carrier, we became best buddies. We hung out together on the porch, and when Maggie came out to sit in her rocking chair, she didn't have hands enough to pet us both.

But Stranger never accompanied me down to Miss G's. He had found a home, and he wasn't about to compromise it. It seemed as if we were cut from the same bolt of cloth when it came to our desire for personal freedom. He was never comfortable in Maggie's house for very long. When she enclosed her backyard for our safety, he paced along the fence line so much that he wore a path where he walked. When his paws got sore and the pads became raw, Maggie realized he would not be satisfied in an enclosure and turned him out again. And so we "outsiders" have remained friends for all these years.

Stranger

Chapter 10
The Shocking Truth

IT WASN'T LONG after Stranger became a permanent resident that Maggie began to notice evidence of other visitors in the area. Her birdfeeders were being robbed, and the galvanized pole they were mounted on was bent down almost to the ground. She suspected that the black bear she'd seen the day before was the perpetrator. She called Draya to help her straighten the pole, and fortunately they were able to fix it almost like new. But the next time the problem occurred, the pole was not so easily straightened, nor was it on the third or fourth time.

At that point, Draya announced that she'd had enough straightening and would fix the problem once and for all. She strode off towards the shed behind her house. I remained with Maggie; it was apparent that she needed my support. I purred loudly to soothe her as she absentmindedly stroked my head. The fact that she was not paying much attention to me told me she had a lot on her mind.

Draya returned shortly, pushing a wheelbarrow. I went right over and stood up on my hind legs to see what she'd brought. The bed of the wheelbarrow was full of long white stakes just like the ones I had seen around Draya's backyard. She had a gray metal box, a slightly larger plastic box, and rolls of different types of wire. The array also included a hammer, two screwdrivers, wire cutters, and a cordless electric drill. From the look on her face, this time she meant business.

Because I had been present when Draya installed the fence in her backyard, I knew the plastic stakes were easy to install. There was no need to dig postholes and no insulated clips to hold the wire in place; the clips were molded into the plastic posts.

Draya went to great lengths to explain to Maggie what she was doing. "A sharpened metal shaft runs through the middle of each stake for strength and sticks out of the bottom below the plastic. You push it into the ground by stepping on the small plastic foot pedal near the lower end. See, it has an inch-long pin on the bottom," she said as she handed a stake to Maggie for inspection. "The pin helps stabilize the post by bracing it against the ground and counteracting the pull of the wire. The five C-shaped brackets on the side of each stake are there to hold the wire to the stake and to keep the wires apart."

"What are the slits on the top of the brackets for?" Maggie looked puzzled as she turned the stake in her fingers to get a better look.

"It allows the wire to slide into the bracket to install, or to tighten it without having to cut the wire."

Although I didn't completely understand, I thought it all sounded pretty nifty myself.

As Draya set the stakes in a ten-foot diameter circle, around the birdfeeder, I investigated the yellow roll with my paw. Phooey, it was plastic and wire, not the limber yellow cord she often used to tie things in her garden. Sometimes she'd drag *that* cord along the ground for me to pounce on.

As soon as all the stakes were set, Draya unpacked a strange-looking metal box with a long black cord attached. Then she picked up the slightly larger, clear heavy-duty plastic box with a hinged lid. I was so intrigued by what she was doing I moved in closer to see for myself. As she placed the metal box inside the plastic box, she told Maggie she planned to use it to weatherproof the metal box, which was a fence charger.

In her usual, doggedly detailed fashion Draya said, "I'll need to fasten the charger inside the plastic box to that wooden post." She pointed to the one above the railing on the front porch. "But before that, I need to drill three holes in the bottom of the plastic box for the wires to pass through when attached to the fence charger. That way, the lid can be securely closed and fastened."

I placed my front paw against the plastic box to show her where I thought she should drill the holes. She smiled as she gently picked me up and placed me down on the floor of the porch—probably so I wouldn't get hurt. Whether she actually took my advice or not, the job got done, and we were both pretty proud of ourselves. In my opinion, two heads are always better than one.

She left one section between the last two posts open to provide a gap for Maggie to get to the birdfeeder. A single-strand gap wire was installed and would be "hot" when hooked with an insulated handle to the loop. The ground wire, a single strand of heavier gauge uncoated wire, ran to a two-foot piece of metal rebar that she had driven into the ground just outside the drip line of the eave of the roof.

Reacting to Maggie's confused expression, Draya explained. "The dirt must always be moist where the rebar is placed to allow the fence charger to function properly. No kidding, in times of extreme drought, you may have to water the iron pin to moisten the soil around it."

All that remained was to plug the black cord into a live receptacle; when done, the orange light on the charger immediately began to flash, signifying it was working.

"Reach over here and grab this wire," Draya said. "I need to see if it is charging or not."

"Not on a bet," Maggie replied, indignant. "I have no intention of being your guinea pig. Test it yourself; after all, you're the designer and installer." They both laughed.

I couldn't understand what all the fuss was about, never having seen such an elaborate setup before. I figured if you were going to spend the time and effort to install it, you certainly should take the time to test it. It was just too uninteresting for me to dwell on, so I hopped up on the porch swing, curled up, and took a nap.

Two days went by without further incident, long enough for Maggie to clean and refill the birdfeeders and suet feeder. On the third day the bear returned to scope out possible rewards. His nose had picked up the scent of the birdseed long before he spied the full feeders; he made a beeline towards them. Stranger and I were warily watching the bear from the relative safety of the rocking chairs on the porch. Though nervous, we were determined to see what would happen next. Our determination and bravado was backed up by our knowledge that Maggie was just inside watching through the picture window herself.

We didn't have long to wait. The bear went right up to the fence where he stopped and stood motionless for about five seconds before the aroma of the seed reached him again. He was obviously perplexed by the new fence, so he decided to give it a good sniff, and in so doing, he touched his nose to the wire. Yikes! Either I imagined it or I saw the spark in broad daylight. It has been said that the most sensitive part of a bear is its nose. By the way he slammed his whole body into reverse—paws and claws finally getting enough traction to throw dirt and grass clods every which way as he backed away from the fence—I guess that's correct. It was probably the fastest he'd moved in years, but I didn't have a chance to ask him.

As Stranger and I shared a chuckle (if you can say that cats chuckle) the bear was long gone back into the woods, mumbling and grumbling as he went. Needless to say, Maggie's fence was a huge success.

Each year a new set of bears show up to challenge the fences at Maggies's and Draya's, but so far they've served their purpose. Only when a limb falls across the wires or the weeds grow up to ground it out, have the bears been successful in breaking into Draya's backyard. The issue is easily fixed with clippers or a weed-eater, or occasionally re-splicing a broken wire. Maggie's fence seems to be vulnerable only when the flow of electricity is interrupted. I certainly have felt safer since it was installed.

However, bears are smart creatures, and they quickly learned if they couldn't get to the birdfeeder they could walk up on Maggie's front porch for a look-see. Right away, Draya arrived with more posts and wire. This time she made a gap across the entrance to Maggie's porch with a single wire across the opening. A sign was hung on the wire in the middle warning that the fence was electric. As long as the gap is closed, it's "hot," and the bears have learned to keep their distance.

Stranger, on the other hand, had a rude awakening when he sauntered up onto the porch with his tail held high. The wire across the gap was plenty high enough for him to easily pass under, though not his tail; when it touched the wire, it fueled his afterburners. He spun around looking for someone to blame, but the other cats were with me inside looking out of the picture window. Feeling highly insulted, he turned around and did it again as he walked off the porch. From then on Stranger has taken great care to lower his tail before entering or leaving the porch. I guess given a little time we all can learn from our mistakes.

Shocking as it was to Stranger to touch his tail to the "hot" wire, it was nothing compared to what can happen to unwitting animals. Electricity is nothing to play with or joke about. Cats and especially kittens or puppies are prone to playing with or chewing on cords; electric cords are no exception. The best prevention is to make them inaccessible, even though that may not always be possible.

I learned from listening to Maggie and Draya as they talked with their friend Bruce that if your pet does chew a live electrical cord and is unable to let it loose, DO NOT TOUCH YOUR PET. You must disconnect the power to that cord by either unplugging it from the socket or throwing the circuit breaker, whichever is the quickest. If you get shocked, you may not be able to help your pet. Whatever you do, do it fast! Seek medical treatment from a veterinarian immediately; time is of the essence in a situation like this.

Teaching kittens and puppies to leave things alone is, of course, the best solution, but I must admit there are some knuckleheads out there that won't listen or learn no matter what. They tend to get into all sorts of mischief when their caregivers aren't watching them every second; especially when the caregivers aren't at home.

From what I've seen at Maggie's and Draya's, crating them when they must be left alone may be the only answer. It certainly doesn't hurt them and provides the time out they may require. Meet their needs by setting out plenty of fresh water in a receptacle they can't turn over, add a litter box for cats and kittens, and return home often enough to allow puppies and dogs to relieve themselves in an appropriate place. A food dish in the crate is another option to consider if a caregiver plans to be gone for an entire day. Kittens and puppies require feeding more frequently than adult cats and dogs. I'll eat anytime I can persuade someone to feed me. I love to eat.

Chapter 11
Ferals Beget Ferals

MISS KITTY LIVED behind a stand-alone restaurant near a shopping mall. At the time she was 100 percent dependent on what she was able to catch and the scraps the staff occasionally put out for her. Pickings sometimes were so poor that she went hungry, but thanks to a plentiful mouse population she didn't starve. If she was pregnant or feeding kittens, it was doubly hard to maintain herself and her kittens too. In the early years, many of the kittens she carried were stillborn or perished due to malnutrition, parasites, and fleas. But she did her best to care for them all.

One day Maggie spied Miss Kitty lurking behind the air-conditioning unit outside the restaurant. Upon inquiring, she learned that Miss Kitty had grown up there and the staff was feeding her despite the owner having forbidden them to do so. Maggie couldn't bear to hear of a cat going hungry, so she went to the grocery store adjacent to the mall and bought cans of wet food, and a large bag of dry cat food. A package of small paper plates, a box of plastic spoons, a roll of paper towels, and a box of quart-size plastic bags for trash, finished the list. She returned and dished up possibly the first real cat food dinner Miss Kitty had ever had. She placed it behind the A/C unit and left, promising Miss Kitty she'd return the next day with more food.

Neither snow nor rain nor heat nor gloom of night prevented Maggie from completing her appointed rounds. Well, the gloom of night maybe, but for two and a half years she fed Miss Kitty every single day. The restaurant, however, did not fare as well and closed soon after Maggie started feeding Miss Kitty and whatever kittens she had at the time.

Miss Kitty was a wily old puss and soon learned to recognize Maggie's car. Early one evening while Maggie was catching a quick bite to eat with a friend at the fast food joint across from the parking lot where Miss Kitty lived, the friend looked out the window. "Maggie," he said, "isn't that the cat you've been feeding?"

Maggie looked out, and sure enough, there was Miss Kitty trotting across the parking lot towards her parked car. Maggie jumped up, excused herself momentarily, took the hamburger patty off the bun, and went outside to meet her. Since it was not the usual feeding station, Miss Kitty was somewhat leery of coming too close; then she heard Maggie's voice and followed her back over to the closed restaurant out of harm's way; there Maggie fed her the burger.

After the restaurant had been shuttered, vagrants moved in. They began to camp out in a sheltered area behind the restaurant where Maggie fed Miss Kitty during inclement weather. After a while it became apparent that this area was no longer safe for either Miss Kitty or Maggie. At this particular time, Miss Kitty had five kittens coming with her to be fed; she had not completely weaned the litter as yet. Although Maggie had previously tried and failed to trap the group, she knew she must find a way to catch them now.

Again Maggie turned to her friend Draya, who was experienced at trapping feral cats. During a period of low "derelict activity," Maggie and Draya set a trap baited with the smelliest fish cat food Maggie could buy; they waited. They were afraid to leave the trap in case the bums showed back up. Within thirty minutes they were rewarded by the sound of the trap being sprung. Miss Kitty and two of her kittens had been caught. They threw a towel over the trap to calm the panicked cats inside, loaded it into Draya's station wagon, and made a hurried trip to the vet.

They'd made a prior arrangement with the local SPCA for a discounted rate for the vet's office to keep the cats overnight and spay or neuter the ones that were caught. All shots, worming, and flea meds would be given at the time of surgery while the cats were still sedated. Because all were feral and it wasn't feasible to return them to the area where they'd been trapped, the veterinary staff had also agreed to keep them until their incisions began to heal.

Maggie and Draya returned to the restaurant with the trap and reset it. They decided it would be safe enough to leave it while they ate at the burger joint. It must have been providence because when they returned, two more little faces were peering out of the trap. Maggie and Draya looked all around but could see no sign of the last kitten. They needed to get the two they had to the vet's office before it closed, as it was getting late. So they picked up the remaining food and left; they planned to return first thing in the morning. The remaining kitten should be hungry by then.

By now I had learned that "first thing in the morning" for Maggie actually meant between nine thirty and ten. Though I should cut her some slack, she worked late at her job and often stayed up until after midnight to unwind from the day's activities. She had to sleep sometime.

In the morning Maggie met Draya, and for the third time they went to the restaurant to set the trap. Because it was a work day, Maggie was anxious for the last kitten to show up quickly. They placed the trap in a spot where the kitten would likely return and slipped the closed end into a brown paper bag; it made the trap less formidable and more inviting. Again they baited it with stinky fish and went away in search of a late breakfast. There was no kitten in the trap when they came back. Discouraged but hopeful, they agreed to try once more the next day. They figured the kitten would really be hungry by then if it was still around.

All was repeated the next morning, and by the time they returned to check the trap, they were successful. The last of the five had been caught. Maggie breathed a long sigh of relief. Off to the vet they went. The kitten had eaten so little once trapped, the vet determined it was OK to neuter the little guy that morning rather than make him fast overnight.

Kittens need to eat often, and adult cats need to eat on a regular basis as well; if they stop eating for a long time, they can get fatty liver disease, which can lead to liver failure. The disease is prevalent in cats that have lost their home or caregivers and are so saddened or stressed that they refuse to eat.

After the kitten's surgery, he was reunited with Miss Kitty and his littermates. Unfortunately, by the end of the week, the vet bill was too high to keep Miss Kitty and her litter there, so they were moved to a boarding facility; Maggie struggled to find homes for them. The major strike against them was that they were all feral. Miss Kitty was so afraid of people that she could not teach her kittens proper manners. All they knew was flight or fight. And as small as they were, they certainly knew how to bite and scratch. It would take a lot of patience to teach them that people could be kind.

A vet from another office agreed to take the two male kittens. He wanted mousers for the barn behind his house. He kept them in the barn for several days in a crate he brought home from the clinic. He fed and watered them daily, but didn't have much time to spend trying to tame them. The minute he released them from the crate into the barn, they took off like they were shot out of a gun, and he never saw them again. I hope they were able to join a feral community in the area and live out their lives peacefully. Who knows; the life expectancy of a feral cat is very limited, about six to seven years at best. These two had a little better chance than most. They had been neutered, vaccinated, wormed, and treated for fleas.

A professional adult sitter who kept Draya's mother for a time before Draya retired offered to take the small gray female, which she named Binky. The woman had just lost a cat she'd adopted a year before. The cat had slipped out of the house when she was going out and didn't return. The next day she discovered it had been hit and killed on her busy street.

Binky was terrified when she first arrived, but the sitter's other cat, Beau, set about teaching Binky to enjoy the woman's company. Her new owner allowed her to discover things for herself and never tried to make Binky like her. As time passed, Beau's calm demeanor, the good food, and her own curiosity helped Binky develop trust in her benefactress.

The other two kittens were eventually placed in homes, but no one ever let Maggie know how the kittens fared. The fate of Miss Kitty was a whole different story. No one wanted to take a chance with her. As much as Maggie was willing to try, she couldn't take the cat because of her work schedule. Maggie finally approached Draya, who agreed to give Miss Kitty a chance. After an introductory period, Draya turned Miss Kitty out into her house. I discovered, after talking to some of the cats that were living in the home when Miss Kitty arrived, that Miss Kitty had a lot to learn. She was a major touch-me-not and would hide all day until suppertime. She did slink around the house at night when everyone else was asleep. The only way Draya could get Miss Kitty into a carrier for a trip to the vet was to catch her in a large fish net. A fight always ensued in trying to get her from the net into the carrier. Once at the clinic, she had to be gassed with nitrous oxide before she could be taken out of the carrier and examined or medicated. It was very hard for everyone involved, but Miss Kitty would hurt anyone trying to handle her otherwise.

On one such occasion, Miss Kitty had been relegated to the carrier and driven to the clinic for her annual checkup and vaccinations. She still exemplified all the feral traits she had when she was first caught. Draya had been in a bit of a hurry when she closed Miss Kitty into the carrier. When they arrived at the clinic, Draya lifted the carrier from the car. Miss Kitty jumped forward, the wire door flew open, and out she shot. Over the lawn and up the bank she ran, disappearing into the neighborhood behind the clinic. The latch on the carrier door had not been properly fastened. Draya ran in to tell the staff what had happened, but there was nothing anyone could do. Miss Kitty was free, and she was not about to come when called.

Miss Kitty escaped on the last warm day in February that year, just before an arctic blast swooped in from Canada and plunged temperatures into the teens. Draya was devastated and worried about Miss Kitty finding a food source. Not knowing which way Miss Kitty went after she ran up the hill, she couldn't establish a feeding station.

Maggie and Draya put out flyers all over the neighborhood. They drove every street in the area for two months but never saw her. Finally, they accepted the fact she was gone and that maybe she was trying to work her way back to the restaurant where she had lived for so many years. They even checked there. Miss Kitty had been wearing a red collar with a rabies tag from the vet's office where she had escaped; they hoped that if she still had it on, whoever saw her would realize that she had had a home at one time and would be kind to her.

Four months almost to the day after Miss Kitty had escaped, Draya was in the grocery store when her cell phone rang. It was the vet's office calling to tell her that a couple who lived in a house near the clinic had found Miss Kitty. When Draya returned the call, the lady told her that there had been a cat squabble the night before; when she and her husband went to see about it, they found a red collar with a tag and the vet's phone number. They suspected a cat had been living under their pottery shed during the cold winter months. They had put out food, which was always consumed, but they never actually saw what ate it.

As the weather began to warm and spring was just around the corner, they started sitting out on their lawn in the evening. A cat with a red collar would come and sniff around for a handout; both assumed it belonged to someone in the neighborhood. It wasn't until the husband found the collar that they had the vet's number to call. It was decided that they'd wait to call Draya again until after they successfully trapped the cat. Three days later the phone rang:

success. Draya thanked the lady and left immediately to see if the cat they had trapped was indeed Miss Kitty. As soon as she turned into the driveway and saw the cat in the trap, she knew it was.

Afraid of losing her again, she asked the lady to loan her the trap Miss Kitty was in so she could take her to the vet. She promised to return it as soon as they could check Miss Kitty's condition. Per usual, Miss Kitty was anesthetized for her exam. She'd lost some weight, but overall she was in great shape. At the vet's office, they transferred Miss Kitty into the carrier Draya had brought with her.

After returning the trap to its owner, Draya took Miss Kitty straight home and put her in a crate for observation. Also, she wanted to be able to easily give Miss Kitty medication or possibly take her back to the vet if all was not well in the next day or so. The next morning when she went to feed her, Miss Kitty was in the front of the cage waiting for her breakfast, and when the cage door was opened to put her food dish in, Miss Kitty leaned forward and rubbed her head against the hand that fed her. It was nothing short of a miracle.

Although Miss Kitty never became a lap cat, she never had to be sedated for an exam again. Miss Kitty lived with Draya until she died due to paralysis caused by toxins in the tail of a blue-tailed skink, which she had eaten. Some folks might argue that there is no such malady, but having watched Miss Kitty stagger around with the telltale head tilt and then fade away as the toxin continued to paralyze her internal organs, I think they are full of baloney. Maggie and Draya did everything they could to save her but to no avail. Rather than have Miss Kitty suffer any longer, they mercifully had her put to sleep, and she crossed over the Rainbow Bridge to join the others that had passed before her. After they brought Miss Kitty home, another grave was added to our cemetery.

As Binky's owner's health declined and she was no longer able to take care of herself or her cats, the house they lived in became a horrific mess. It was deemed necessary by the woman's family to remove the cats. A niece knew that Binky had come from Maggie and asked her to take the cats; Maggie agreed.

Because of Binky's feral background, Maggie was afraid she would not fit into her home situation, so Draya agreed to take both Beau and Binky. Unfortunately, she lost Beau within a month to a clot that had suddenly formed in his pelvic region, stopping the blood flow to his hind legs. Before she could get him to the vet's office, he was gone. As has been noted before, things happen.

Binky adores her new home with Draya. She has a back deck and patio that she shares with the other cats in the house. They all enjoy a fenced grass yard with shrubs to sleep under and trees to climb, and their very own koi pond with two waterfalls. The six-foot chain link fence is topped with netting and flexible stanchions that most cats are afraid to climb. And there's netting over the pond to keep any cats who're tempted to "fish" at bay. A cat door installed in a window allows access to the deck day or night. Binky has blossomed into a very calm and loving cat and seems to get along with every cat that passes through our home. We've become best pals. It was she who told me her mom's story.

Binky

Chapter 12
Brave Heart

WHEN MAGGIE FIRST saw William Wallace, he was just a little kitten about three months old. He was living with a husband and wife dedicated to rescuing feral cats, and he was one of their rescues.

William had been born under a large brush pile in the middle of a field that was being cleared by a farmer for crop planting. He was only two or three days old when the landowner decided to get rid of the pile by burning it. Whether or not the man knew the mother cat and her kittens were in the brush pile when he lit it is a matter between him and his God.

As the dry brush caught fire, the mother cat ran out with William in her mouth. She went a short distance away from the pile and dropped him on some grass. Then she darted straight back into the burning pile to get another kitten. A gust of wind came up, and the pile instantly became an inferno. Neither the mother cat nor any of the other kittens survived.

William's eyes were still closed, and a short, dried piece of umbilical cord was still attached to his belly when he was found squirming in the patch of grass. His rescuers had experience in raising orphaned newborn kittens, so he received the round-the-clock attention he so desperately needed. Fortunately, he had nursed long enough to get enough colostrum, which the mother produces in the first few days of lactation. Colostrum is essential for boosting the immune system into action.

However, because his mom had been a feral cat and never received vaccinations or immunizations, William would suffer the consequences. By the time his eyes opened, he was full of worms and had a lot of fleas. They wormed him, but he was still too young to treat for fleas the traditional way, so his caregivers combed and handpicked the fleas off of him. He had to be bottle fed and had no mom to snuggle up to for warmth, no mom to bathe him or give him comfort. At a time when he so desperately needed one, there were no surrogate moms around. So he was poked, prodded, and dosed with nasty-tasting medicines, and he grew to despise it. Against all the odds, he survived infancy and turned out to be a super cute kitten.

By the time he reached two months old, he was allowed supervised play on the patio outside of the couple's mountain home. He loved to investigate every new leaf that fell or anything else that might be found. The smell of the damp earth and stones exhilarated him, and he delighted in being alive and outside. He had two speeds: stopped and wide open. He tore around with total abandon. He was a mess.

Maggie was so taken by this kitten that she sent food, toys, and treats to him every week for several months. She talked nonstop about him and the things William had done when she first saw him. Maggie was so captivated; it was as if she were bewitched. But, alas, William had also charmed his caregivers and was not available for adoption.

I've lived long enough to know that some adages and old wives' tales often hold more truth than poetry. "Be careful what you wish for, for wishes can come true," is a case in point. Almost six months to the day after they had visited the feral cat sanctuary, Draya received a phone call from the wife of the owner asking if she would take two hard-to-place cats: Tony and Gidget. Both were feral tripods (three-legged) and not easily relocated.

The male, Tony, because he had been shot and lost his hind leg, was quite shy around people. Gidget, a tiny little cat, lost her leg after being hit by a car. She had patches of skin where the hair never re-grew, and because of her looks, she was also not likely to be adopted. Gidget was one of the cutest, sweetest cats I had ever met;

she'd long since lost any feral tendencies she might have once possessed.

"My husband's taken a new job in the eastern part of the state, and we have to move," the lady said with regret. "We can take some, but not all of our rescued cats and we're seeking good homes for the ones we have to leave behind."

"What are your plans for William Wallace?" asked Draya, but the wife said that William was one of the cats they planned to take with them. "If you change your mind, let me know," Draya said before she hung up the phone.

A week after Draya had taken possession of Tony and Gidget, the lady called again, this time to say that if Maggie still wanted William Wallace, they would like for her to have him. She said, "Things have changed, and we won't be able to take as many of our cats as we first planned. We know Maggie will give our William Wallace an exceptionally good home."

Draya said "Yes!" without hesitation, knowing Maggie's response would be the same. It was agreed that the couple would bring William to town the next day. Draya couldn't wait to tell Maggie.

Though William came into Maggie's house as a youngster, he made it clear within a very short time that he didn't want to be an inside cat. Maggie thought I would be a good teacher and companion for him. I took him to Miss G's when I knew she would be working in the garden. But William was too young to enjoy the simple pleasures of gardening, quickly became bored, and began to wander down the street.

I'd been down that road before and had no desire to leave my comfortable surroundings for another walk on the wild side. William, however, could not be dissuaded, so I wished him good luck and returned to Miss G's. From that day until this past bitterly cold and snowy winter, he'd traipse off daily to some unknown place but was always home for supper. The influence of his feral background must have been very intense to draw him away from the security Maggie provided; after all, he was still just a kitten.

One evening William didn't return for supper as usual. Maggie was beside herself with worry. She and Draya searched up and down our street, calling his name as they went. Every so often they would stop and listen. Maggie thought she could hear his cries, but each time they stopped calling to listen, they were met with silence.

"He's still so little," Maggie said with a sniffle. "If anything has happened to him I'll blame myself forever. Whatever can I do? Wait! Listen! Do you hear that?" she added in a whisper. They both looked into the dark woods and strained to listen, hoping to hear sounds from him. No small mews were heard.

That night it poured rain but stopped raining by mid-morning. Maggie and Draya were back out pounding the pavement shortly after dawn. By the time they returned to Maggie's front porch, they were soaked to the skin and complaining bitterly about the inadequacy of modern day rain apparel. The manufacturer had marked it rainproof but had neglected to mention the period of time it actually repelled water. I think that their complaints were just a cover for their worry about William.

It continued to rain off and on for the next three days; still no sign of William. The ladies discussed thinking they'd heard him meowing from time to time but couldn't locate the direction the cries were coming from. They also admitted that what they thought they heard might just be wishful thinking.

The evening of the fourth day, when all seemed lost and hopelessness had begun to set in, Maggie asked her boss if she could leave work early to look for William. He agreed. She called Draya to tell her what she was planning and left work an hour and a half early. She hurried home, parked her car, got out with a flashlight in hand, and strode off down the street. Twenty minutes later she came running up the street to find Draya. "I found him; I found William Wallace," she screamed through laughter and tears of happiness.

"Do you have him? Where is he?" Draya shouted before running from the house to meet Maggie.

"You'll never in a hundred years believe this; I'll just have to show you." Almost out of breath, Maggie dashed back down the street. Draya, for once, was having trouble just keeping pace.

Maggie stopped right in front of Miss G's driveway but pointed her flashlight to the middle of the empty fenced lot across the street. Flipping the flashlight on, Maggie aimed the beam toward the middle of the lot. "There," she said.

"Where?" Draya strained to see what the bobbing beam was supposed to illuminate.

"There," Maggie said, pointing again. "No, no, not there . . . follow the beam."

Draya's eyes followed the beam of light as it traveled up the trunk of a very large oak tree to the first limb. "Mew," came the very weak cry from up the tree. "Mew. Mew."

As Draya's eyes scanned the tree, she finally spotted the weak, tired kitten. "William Wallace, how in the devil did you manage to get up there?" Looking down the side of the tree to the base of the trunk, she estimated the tree to be approximately a hundred feet tall and at least three feet in diameter. The limb William sat on had to be all of thirty feet from the ground. He would have had to climb the tree straight up like a squirrel. But how he got up there was not the problem. The problem was how to get him down.

Years before Draya moved to our neighborhood; her dad had purchased a thirty-two-foot extension ladder that she had used at her farm while rebuilding a barn. Although she had climbed it many times in the past, years had gone by, and she was no longer able to climb a ladder that tall; her knees just wouldn't hold her.

William was frantic in his desire to get to them; they feared he might fall trying to come down on his own. Something had to be done and soon. Draya's greatest fear was that climbing the ladder might spook William, causing him to climb even higher. There were no cat rescuers that she knew of that climbed trees in the daytime, let alone in the middle of the night.

Suddenly she was struck by an idea. Draya took out her cell phone and called a friend who would be getting ready to close his Thai restaurant for the night. He was fearless when it came to heights and extremely agile. Following her brief description of the current dilemma, he agreed to help.

Time passes excruciatingly slowly when you are awaiting a rescue. While Maggie cleared the brush and briars from around the base of the tree, Draya returned home for a cat carrier, a small duffel bag, and the ladder. Fortunately, the ladder was right where she thought it would be, but she realized that it was too heavy for her to lift by herself. She'd need to have her friend help her carry it to the site. By the time Draya returned to the tree, Maggie had finished clearing a space for them to work and her friend had just pulled up in his van.

"Keep driving up to my shed," Draya said before he could open the door. "We need to get my big ladder." She walked back to her house as he positioned the van and opened the top hatch in the back door. Together they lifted the ladder and slid it in over the top of the seats all the way to the dashboard and up against the inside of the windshield. The ladder stuck out the rear hatch for more than half its length.

When they got to the tree, Draya and her friend struggled to unload the ladder and work it through the only gate in the fence. Maggie had gone to get another flashlight. Its stronger light beam revealed that William Wallace was still up the tree and that he was becoming quite agitated. William nearly took their breath away when he started pacing up and down the limb he was on. A thirty-foot fall and he might have been history.

All the noise they were making awakened me. I had been asleep in a snuggly cozy on Maggie's porch. I got out of the cozy and went down the street to watch what was happening from the security of

Miss G's driveway. That was when I saw William high up in the tree. What will that kitten do next? I pondered as I watched and waited.

Draya and her friend struggled to extend the ladder up the tree. It was now rapidly approaching midnight. Finally, the ladder was extended as far as they dared and was placed as securely as they could manage against the trunk of the tree. However, the top rung was still two feet below the bottom of the first limb, the limb where William was crouched and peering down at them. As feared, when they placed the ladder, William got spooked; for a terrifying moment they thought he might climb even higher to the next limb. That would have put him totally out of reach. But with both women calling to him, William decided to stay where he was.

Draya explained her plan to her friend. "Once you climb to a place where you can reach William, you'll only have one chance to get a hold of him. You'll need to reach over his back or head, depending on which way he's facing, and grab him by the scruff of his neck. Then pick him up off the limb, zip him into the duffel bag, and climb back down the ladder. Maggie will transfer William from the duffel bag to the carrier and take him home."

Instructions understood, and with time being of the essence, Draya's friend shouldered the duffel bag, tested the ladder, and began his ascent. Halfway up he paused to look up and locate William, who was watching from the crook of the limb straight above him.

Maggie and Draya softly spoke encouraging words from below as Draya's friend reached the top of the ladder. A quick assessment confirmed the need for accuracy as well as speed. As he grabbed for the kitten's scruff, the ladder readjusted slightly under his weight. Both Maggie and Draya jumped forward and grabbed the ladder on both sides to steady it. William was flailing the air with all four feet. Afraid his hold was not good enough, the man "velcroed" William to the side of the tree.

William clung to the trunk with his tiny claws, still thirty feet above the ground, as Draya's friend adjusted his grip. He swung the duffel bag off his shoulder and against the top of the ladder, and shoved William headfirst into the bag. Down they came with William's hind end hanging out of the bag; he was kicking and squirming. To speed things up, Draya's friend put both of his feet on the outside of the ladder and slid the remaining way down. Everyone let out big sighs of relief when they reached the ground.

Maggie grabbed the bag, withdrew a trembling William, and cradled him in her arms. "How in the world did you get into such a fix, you little scamp?" she asked.

Draya and her friend were busy taking down the ladder and picking up the tools. Draya needed to move the ladder back to her house while she still had help available. William was placed into the carrier, and I accompanied them back to Maggie's house. As we walked away, we could hear Draya thanking her friend profusely for saving the day.

Back at our house, Maggie fed William his first meal in four days. She and Draya speculated about why and how the kitten had managed to climb straight up that huge tree. The only plausible scenario they came up with was that the neighbors' daughter and her boyfriend had brought their two dogs with them when they came to visit her parents. Neither of the dogs was well trained, and both were very aggressive. The girl's mother refused to let the dogs in her house, so it was the boyfriend's habit to turn them loose in the vacant fenced lot. William must have been inside the fence looking around when the dogs arrived. Most likely the dogs chased poor little William, and a surge of adrenaline—brought on by sheer terror—sent him straight up that tree!

If that sounds familiar, I had had that sort of feeling when I fled from my first home in a total panic. But how William managed to make it all the way up to that limb so high off the ground can only be chalked up to Providence. Let's just say the alternative was not an option. The feat was equivalent to a man climbing the outside of the Empire State Building without any ropes or pulleys. Well, maybe not quite, but you get my drift. Also, I think the only reason William survived for four days was that it rained every day and he was able to lap up some of the rainwater.

Although we may never know the absolute truth of the matter, it is worth noting that in his many years of living here and with all the wandering around the neighborhood he's done, William has never set a paw in that lot again. William's oak tree still stands as a testament to what can be accomplished given a particular set of circumstances.

William's Tree

Chapter 13
Furever Friends

After Maggie had lost Wendell, Wendy, and Rascal, she adopted several more cats—some adult cats and an occasional kitten or two. I was there to show them the ropes as best I could. She had already enclosed her backyard to keep out predators as well as to keep her cats in. Maggie long ago realized that indoor-only cats were much safer than outdoor cats. By fencing the area, her cats could experience fresh air and nature with less risk. She patterned the fencing after the backyard enclosure at Draya's. But Stranger, William Wallace, and I were just too used to our personal freedom to submit to being shut in. After all, I needed to be at Miss G's regularly for garden chores and snacks.

Maggie and Draya began attending the weekend cat adoption days run by friends who had cat shelters in our area. They went to lend support and to visit with friends. It was during one of these visits that Maggie learned of a tragic occurrence involving two lovely cats. Both cats—one a pastel tortoiseshell domestic long hair, and the other a dark tortoiseshell domestic short hair—had been declawed on all four paws. (The tortoiseshell and calico coats are gender specific to females. In extremely rare cases a male will be born with calico coloring. Usually they're sterile and almost never live past their first year.)

The issue of whether to declaw or not is hotly debated these days among cat lovers, lawmakers, and veterinarians. It's generally thought that there are pros and cons, but in my humble opinion declawing is a barbaric practice—unless it's medically necessary. Not only is the claw surgically removed, but also in many if not most cases, the first bone on each toe is removed with it. Worse still, if the person doing the declawing is not extremely careful or is somehow distracted, sometimes half of the second bone is lopped off as well. If improperly done, the cat may spend the rest of its life in excruciating pain, though you may never know it, as we cats are extremely good at hiding our pain. Even if done with care, some cats never get over the tenderness in their toes and remain skittish about having them touched. Many are so resentful that they become biters.

What happened to these two loving cats after they had been declawed was inconceivable. The cats' owners decided they no longer wanted them and turned them outside with no way to feed or defend themselves. Fortunately, a kind soul found the pastel tortoiseshell—who was sick and starving—and had the compassion to take her to a vet clinic. A neighbor had found the other cat in his backyard and brought her to the adoption days. Maggie immediately agreed to take them so she could give them a good home. Shadow and Annie are now permanent residents at Maggie's.

I have had the pleasure of making their acquaintance. The larger dark one, Annie, is a real talker; she can bend your ear for hours if you let her. Although declawed on all four paws, she told me of her resolve not to become a biter. She figured if her owners were so paranoid about her damaging their things with her claws that they removed all of them, then what might be removed if she bit someone. She definitely had a point.

Annie also confided in me that when her elderly owners died, the family came in from out of town, took what they wanted, and disposed of the rest within a week. Nobody in the family wanted a cat, so Annie was turned outside, the consensus being that the neighbors would look after her. They didn't look for her records, nor did they pay the slightest attention to the fact that she had been declawed. They just put her out in the backyard, locked up the now empty house, and left. No water or food was put out to tide her over. Annie was totally bewildered, but within the hour she was fleeing for her life; the neighbor's dog found her and chased her up a tree.

"It's hard to climb a tree without any claws," she related. "The surge of adrenaline I got from sheer terror did amazing things, and up that tree I went. The dog's owner didn't find me for two days, and I stayed right where I was; I knew that the dog had all the advantage if I fell out of the tree. Finally I just gave in and meowed all my sorrow. The dog heard me first and stood up against the tree barking menacingly at me. His owner finally appeared to see what the ruckus was all about. The dog was not about to hush with me still in the tree, so his owner investigated and found me, scared speechless, clinging to a limb. I'd only been able to climb just above the dog's reach, still well within reach of the man. At that point I didn't know who or what to trust, so I just hung onto the branch with all my toes.

"The man quickly put his dog in the house and returned with a bowl of milk. 'You must be thirsty,' he said as he held the bowl up to me. I was too afraid I'd fall if I tried to drink it, so he put the bowl down and calmly reached up and pried me off of the limb. He then said, 'What in the world? How could anyone just turn you loose?' Shock registered on his face as he realized that I was totally declawed.

"I snuggled close to his chest before he gently put me down on the ground. I sniffed the bowl of milk. It was not my choice—I'd never had cow's milk before—but it was wet, and I was so thirsty I quickly lapped the bowl dry. I stood my ground as he reached down to pick up the bowl, but then I rubbed my head lightly against his hand to thank him. He was clearly in a quandary when he reached for the bowl. I could tell by the way he looked at me he was debating what to do next. He started to go back inside his house and I tried to follow. 'Oh no,' he firmly said as he blocked my entering with his leg. 'Bruno would eat you for breakfast if I let you in. Wait here. I'll get you something more to eat.'

"What he brought was edible, but barely: a plate of canned dog food and, thank the stars, a bowl of cool, fresh water. As hungry as I was, pride was not going to stand in my way; I chowed down. I couldn't eat it all, though; the milk had almost filled my belly. I quenched what thirst I had left with the water, washed my face, and then stretched out on his back steps to relax for the first time in what seemed like forever.

"No sooner did I get comfortable than out of the house the man came again, talking a mile a minute on his cell phone. It sounded to me like he was getting directions to somewhere. Back into the house he went. Several minutes later he reappeared carrying a roll of tape and a cardboard box with small holes cut in the side. Before I could inquire or complain, I was scooped up and deposited into the box. He quickly closed the lid and applied the tape. He muttered something about it being Saturday and an adoption event nearby as he placed the box in his car.

"And that's how I met Maggie. The rest of my saga remains to be seen." Annie sighed heavily.

Shadow, on the other hand, has never spoken about the circumstances that brought her to the animal rescue center. All I know is that Maggie told Draya that Shadow was found lying on the side of the road, emaciated and covered with fleas. Half dead, she was taken to a vet clinic where they gave her fluids and a rabies vaccination. They also wormed her, treated her flea infestation, and called a rescue cattery to pick her up.

The director of the cattery paid the vet bill and took her back to the shelter for rehabilitation until Shadow was well enough to be put up for adoption. It had taken a full three weeks before she was ready for the adoption day event; it was on that same day that Annie was brought in by the neighbor. Maggie ended up taking both of them home with her that afternoon.

"You are going to be my new best friends; you will stay with me forever. That makes us 'furever' friends," Maggie cooed to them as she and Draya drove home. "Your lives will be much simpler now."

I've often tried to get Shadow to tell me her story, but she just looks at me with her sad green eyes and doesn't say anything. Her trauma must be so deep-seated that she either can't or won't talk about it. She does, however, have a holdover from the terrible flea infestation she suffered. Shadow now has a major allergy to fleas, so in addition to administering monthly flea medication, Maggie must take her to get regular allergy shots to keep her from scratching her face, neck, and ears raw.

If you feel you must declaw a cat to be able to have one in your home, then be responsible enough to recognize how vulnerable you've made that cat to potentially dangerous situations. You'll need to provide secure shelter, food, and water at all times; letting it outside without protection will no longer be an option.

Shadow is learning to trust and has given her allegiance to Maggie. Shadow follows her everywhere in the house and even sleeps on her bed. Her coat is filling in with healthy silky hair, and she's gained weight. Best of all, the sadness is beginning to fade from her eyes.

Chapter 14
Homeward Bound

I KNEW FROM conversations I'd overheard that the ladies who took care of me were not happy with my outdoor-oriented life. Age had slowed my walk and reaction time, and the effects of the weather were harder on my body. The cold acutely affected my arthritis, and I began to seek heat by lying in a sunny spot in the middle of our street. My hearing was not as good as it had been, so when a car approached, I didn't always hear it until it was nearly on top of me. Fortunately for me, the drivers on our street were familiar with my habit and gave me time to move out of the way. However, visitors and drivers of commercial vehicles were not aware of my habit and often had to brake sharply; I shudder even now to think of some of the near misses.

Miss G tried to convince me to stay in her house, and I did for a while. She made special boxes lined with old towels or rugs strategically placed around the first floor of her home. But I still had an aversion to using an indoor litter box, so when I needed to, I went to the door and asked politely to be let out, usually between 10:00 p.m. and 3:00 a.m. It was an obvious annoyance to Miss G and her daughter, Jan, (when Jan came to visit her parents) to have to get out of bed to let me out.

The other challenge to my living indoors at Miss G's was Harry. Age had made him very unsteady on his feet, even though he still took daily walks around the neighborhood. Outside he used two long walking sticks to aid his balance; as long as he kept walking and didn't stop, the rhythm of his stride kept him from losing his balance. He was a bit like a motorcycle; when moving forward at a decent speed it will stay upright, but slowed down or stopped it will fall over if not supported.

Maggie and Draya saw him walking outside often when they were going out or coming back from running errands. They marveled that Harry had never fallen, and always drew a quick breath whenever he almost did. He was an accident waiting to happen.

Inside the house, Harry was forced to move among the furniture at a much slower pace without the aid of his sticks, and being very tall he was at a greater risk of falling. The fact that I was often underfoot and not as agile as I once was caused many near mishaps. Miss G worried about it constantly and would always try to make sure I was out of the way before Harry entered the room. Worry finally took its toll on her, and without a choice, I was again relegated to being an outdoor cat.

Even though Miss G felt it was safer because of my being a tripping hazard, she couldn't bear the thought of me enduring another winter outside in the cold. So she persuaded Jan to ask Jerry—the contractor who built the new garage and addition to the house—to design and build a snuggly warm house just for me. Talk about being privileged; I strutted around for days, tail and nose held high, showing off for anyone who would take notice of my new personal digs.

My house was erected on four posts about three feet off the ground. It boasted two doors so I wouldn't be hemmed in if some uninvited creature came calling. I could access it using a ramp that led from the ground to the wraparound porch. It was designed to resemble Miss G's house (given some poetic license) and was painted white with green trim and shingles to match. Inside, several layers of soft blankets—carefully folded to avoid wicking any moisture from the outside—provided padding for my old bones. It was a dream house, and I used it night and day, rain or shine.

"Place it in the front yard just outside the window of my mom's room," Jan told Jerry. "I hope she'll stop fretting so much about

Senator if she can look out of her window and see him warm and safe."

I tried to oblige by staying in my house when I knew Miss G was in her room. I liked to look in the window to see her too.

Once the house was in place, William Wallace stopped by a few times to check it out, but he soon got the message that I had no intention of sharing and went about his business. Oh, I suppose I would have let him come in if it had been really cold and rainy, but fortunately, it never came to that when he was nearby.

When I finally became an indoor-only cat at Draya's, Jan enclosed a portion of her backyard with a cat proof fence. She had Jerry move my little house there to accommodate her other cats. They play in it from time to time, but as far as I know, no one has claimed it. Pity—though I understand; the feeling of pride in knowing it was built just for you is not there for them.

Chapter 15
Here Today and Gone Tomorrow

ONE BEAUTIFUL LATE afternoon, I'd accompanied Maggie to the front porch where she was enjoying the cool breeze from the comfort of her rocking chair. Some time previously I'd appointed myself security guard to watch for whatever moved while she lost herself in the pages of a magazine. There'd been a momma bear with three cubs sniffing around her house a little more than usual. When a strange white cat appeared in the yard, I went immediately to investigate. We squared off at a safe distance. "Who are you and where did you come from?" I asked with a growl, standing my ground on the stone walkway.

The youngster cocked his head down, arched his back, and lowered his tail to wrap it around his body. The only movement he made, other than his jaw when he talked, was the angry lashing of his tail. He clearly had been surprised to see me come off the porch, and his body language told me he didn't like surprises. I guessed him to be about two to three years old, and very full of himself. A casual observer might have assumed he was an intact Tom passing through. But somehow I didn't think so; his head and body were too slender. He didn't possess that large blocky head with muscular jaws, thick neck, and powerful shoulders most often associated with an intact male cat.

In my opinion, he was just a wannabe Tom that had already been neutered, although he could have been a *crypt orchid* (a condition in which one testicle is retained high in the body, therefore not removed in surgery, and still producing hormones), which might have explained his haughty temperament. At this point, looking back, one can only guess.

My second guess then was that he was extremely hungry, much like I was so many years ago when I first came to Maggie's house. I was just about to suggest he cool it, that I'd share my supper with him, when he replied to my initial question.

"My name is none of your business," he said with a snarl. "Are you so old and blind you didn't see me come out of the woods? Out of the woods is where I came from, old puss." His sassy reply was just what you might expect from an undisciplined teenager.

I hadn't intended for our conversation to become so quickly heated, but we had managed to get Maggie's attention.

"Hey, what's going on here?" she asked in a stern voice. "Stop it, both of you!"

He was gone in a flash. I waited to see if he would reappear. He didn't, so I returned to Maggie's side. She was up peering over the railing in the direction he had fled.

"I don't think I've seen that one before. Have you, Senator?" she said, still looking for the cat.

I didn't answer. I didn't have to; she knew I hadn't.

It was Maggie's habit to put food out for the opossums that had survived the trapping during the great raccoon invasion. I'd already said goodnight and had gone back down the street to Miss G's for supper and our evening get-together with Miss G and Harry in their den. That night, when Maggie started out to leave a plate of leftovers and dry dog food for the opossums, she caught a glint of white under the holly bush beside the walk.

"I'll just bet that's the new cat and I'll wager he's hungry," she murmured under her breath, not wanting to scare him again. Maggie quickly retraced her steps back into the house and returned with another plate, this one filled with cat food. Stepping off the porch, she placed the food near the holly bush and continued to the birdfeeder with the opossum food, which she set down near the base of the feeder. Backing away from the house, Maggie watched the plate of food by the holly. Several minutes passed, but her patience was rewarded when slowly and cautiously the white cat snuck out toward the plate. At first he would grab a bite, then dart back to his hiding place under the bush. But as hunger won out over fear, he ate the remaining food in huge gulps until it was all gone. He probably would have licked the plate clean, but his fear returned and he disappeared into the darkness.

"Poor thing," Maggie said, sighing. "His white coat has probably been a detriment to him his whole life. It's like he can't go anywhere or do anything without the risk of being seen. Well, good night, little kitty, wherever you've gone. There will be breakfast in the morning if you want to join us." Her voice trailed off as she went in, turned off the lights, and went to bed.

He didn't show up first thing the next morning, though I was certainly there to check on things. I could tell that he had been back; I could smell him. He'd gone to the trouble of spraying the bushes to make his presence known. That was a practice I had never stooped to; I made my presence known by just being there.

When he did return it was late, and Maggie was again feeding the opossums. She marveled at how incredibly white he was, especially when he moved into the light from the closest streetlight. He was white as the driven snow, and from then on Maggie called him Snowflake. She went to get his dinner.

This time Snowflake didn't hide under the holly bush; neither did he come running up to her when she returned with his food. He just stood at the end of the walk and watched her. Only when Maggie had placed the plate of food on the walk and retreated to the porch did Snowflake approach the dish. He ate in a more genteel manner this time, savoring each bite instead of gobbling it down. He still seemed very leery and looked as if he might flee at a moment's notice, but he was a bit more relaxed than he'd been the night before.

When he'd finished the food Maggie provided for him, Snowflake looked up and stared straight into her eyes. It was his way of thanking her for his dinner. The porch light illuminated him almost as well as daylight would.

"I'll be darned," Maggie said. "You're not only solid white, but you're an odd-eyed cat as well." Her comment referred to his one yellow eye and one blue eye. Aware that most blue-eyed white cats are predisposed to being deaf she queried, "I wonder if you can hear with the ear on your blue-eyed side. It's no wonder you're so jumpy."

Given time, Snowflake began to relax and settle into the neighborhood. He started to follow me down to Miss G's and back, though he still made other side trips on his own as well. Where he went was of no concern to me, but his newfound voracious appetite for human companionship finally got Snowflake into trouble.

He'd developed the habit of biting or grabbing a human arm or leg and holding on with his claws if he felt he wasn't getting enough attention. He wasn't mean or sneaky, just overly reactive to stimulation. Maggie's neighbors were becoming afraid of Snowflake, and Miss G's daughter, Jan, frankly stated she didn't want him around anymore. He was also becoming aggressive toward other cats on our street; it was apparent he was vying for the top cat position. Snowflake was becoming a bully!

Maggie and Draya put their heads together, and Draya agreed to bring him inside her house with her cats to try to rehabilitate him. At first she kept him in a crate so they all could get used to each other's smells and voices. Snowflake was very docile and shy while he was isolated, but the minute he was released into the house, his good manners were forgotten. He challenged everyone, the females included. He quickly found the cat door to the enclosed backyard and passed through. Outside, he paced the fence for a long time, checking every nook and cranny. Not content with being simply outside, Snowflake wanted the complete freedom of going beyond the fence. Both day and night, he made everyone's life miserable. Even Draya's top cat, Meezer, gave him a wide berth. Eventually, Draya and Maggie concluded that the only solution was to find a safe place for him outdoors, somewhere that he would have contact with very few or no other cats but with adequate shelter. A barn would be ideal, with the stipulation that he would be fed and watered once or, even better, twice a day.

Katy, a friend of Maggie and Draya's, had always been amused by Snowflake's antics whenever she came to visit. She empathized with Snowflake's totally independent nature. Katy and her husband, Dan, lived on seven acres in the country with an African gray parrot named Echo and a miniature Sicilian donkey named Penelope. They had had horses in the past, but Penelope was now the only resident of their multi-stall barn. If Katy would agree to take Snowflake as a mouser-in-residence, they figured it might be a win-win situation for all.

It was decided that Penelope would have a new roommate on a trial basis. Draya suggested that Snowflake be kept in a large crate until he adjusted to the sounds and smells of the barn. This arrangement would give Snowflake a chance to get to know Katy better before she turned him loose. It would be a week or so before Snowflake would be released to come and go during the day at will. Even so, he would be fed morning and evening in the crate and locked in it at night. Because Katy worked the evening shift and occasionally double shifts, she typically got up late and returned home late. Everyone agreed that Snowflake would be fed before she left for work and again when she returned home, which was usually after 11:00 p.m. It was a routine Snowflake preferred anyway. The big question on everyone's mind was: would he return after the first time he was released?

The week passed quickly as Katy learned about Snowflake's likes and dislikes and with Snowflake learning to trust and rely on Katy. She was the sole provider of food, water, companionship, and attention. Snowflake reveled in the undivided attention. Katy picked a day when she was off from work to release him from his crate for the first time. She was a little nervous as she opened the door and set his food dish down and waited. Snowflake walked over and sniffed the food but ignored the open door. He took a bite or two of food then turned to face the opening. He didn't bolt but stepped through the door looking at her expectantly.

"I know this may sound weird, but I honestly think he was looking for me to pet his head or rub his tummy," Katy said later. "And when I didn't do it and turned away to go wash his bowl and get fresh water for him out of the spigot, he ran over and grabbed my leg with his front paws and bit me on the calf. He did let go right away, and turned around and went back into the crate to finish the remainder of his breakfast. I was more surprised than hurt. It was evident he felt I'd slighted him and he didn't like it one bit."

Draya asked Katy if she wanted her to come pick Snowflake up to take him back.

"Heavens no," Katy said. "He cracks me up. He left the stall when I left, but he was back for supper at eleven that night. He even jumped up on the stall door and back down inside because I didn't open it fast enough, I guess. Being out of the crate had made him hungry, so he went straight into his crate and drank some water. By that time I had placed his food dish inside the crate, and he chowed down. I decided to close him in for the night and left. He seemed very content to be back in a safe spot where he could sleep with both eyes closed."

Never having been to Katy's place myself, all I could do was listen in on what was being said about my former friend's daily doings. Katy called Draya each night when she got home to relay Snowflake's daily progress and ask questions about his actions. Draya dutifully recapped to Maggie what Katy had told her as they sat for meals at Draya's kitchen table.

Shortly thereafter, Katy introduced Snowflake to Penelope. Penelope, used to being alone at the barn, chose to ignore him completely. Snowflake, wanting to assert his authority, chose that moment to chide her about the noisy racket she made whenever her stall door was opened. He wanted to tell her that she needed to oil her squeaky throat, so he walked over to say his piece. Penelope whirled around, her long ears flattened to her neck and her teeth bared; she lowered her head and charged straight at him. Snowflake looked like someone had grabbed him by his extra-long tail and jerked him inside out as he jumped out of her way and fled back to the safety of his stall. Penelope lost all interest in Snowflake the minute he vanished from her sight; her bray sounded like raspy laughter as she trotted off toward the bottom pasture.

Snowflake consoled his frayed nerves with a dirt bath on the stall floor. He must have felt lucky to be in one piece. That creature was the biggest, strangest looking and sounding dog he'd ever seen.

Snowflake's bravado on several occasions prompted Katy to change his name. She now refers to him as "the Flake Man." Each day they follow a routine of her feeding him and letting him in or out of the crate twice each day. There's no telling what adventures he encounters during the day, but Katy's husband says the Flake Man spends at least part of the day on the deck at their house. Dan has even been suckered into giving tummy rubs on occasion. The Flake Man is no fool.

The Flake Man

Chapter 16
Inherent Danger

IT'S ONLY NATURAL for children to be as active as they are given the freedom to be. It's also natural for a baby or child to flail around even if they have something in their hand. The danger lies in the potential harm that object can do. So parents should teach their small children not to run or play with sharp objects. Letting them do so creates a scenario fraught with danger that can lead to disaster.

So it was that a family with a quiet, gentle Persian cat found instant grief. The mother had been trimming family pictures that she was piecing together as a collage; her two-year-old was playing on the floor beside her, entertaining herself with the picture scraps her mother placed there for her enjoyment. As the saying goes, "All was quiet on the Western Front" until the phone rang. When the mother got up to retrieve her cell phone from the kitchen, she left everything she was working with on the dining room table, with the chair pulled out.

Normally the child would have been content with the bits and pieces her mom had already given her, but curiosity—enhanced by the opportunity granted by her mom's absence—inspired her to climb onto the chair; it gave the child access to everything within her reach on the table. The first thing to catch her eye was a bright red ruler her mom was using to center pictures on the scrapbook page. The girl picked it up, looked it over, stuck it in her mouth, and bit down hard. Apparently, she didn't like the taste or the feel because she jerked it out of her mouth and threw it on the floor. The next thing to be tossed was the bottle of glue, which fortunately still had the cap screwed on tightly.

The child was starting to back down off the chair when she spied the pair of shiny metal scissors partly hidden under the assorted pictures. Back up she went and stood on the chair seat to grab the scissors, which she then threw onto the floor. Specially designed for cutting paper and scrapbooking, the scissors had long thin blades with very sharp points and large finger loops. The rigid blades meshed tightly together and stayed closed if dropped or carelessly laid down.

When the child climbed back off the chair to totter over to the scissors, they were still tightly closed. Reaching down to retrieve them, she teetered off balance and plopped down right on her diaper-covered tush. She giggled happily as she reached out to grab the scissors with one hand.

The family cat—a small, strikingly beautiful longhaired Persian with a dark tortoiseshell coat and pumpkin-colored eyes, had been napping in an adjacent room when she heard the array of objects hit the floor. Curious about what was happening, she went to investigate. She was a sweet, trusting cat that would never intentionally hurt the child. As she came up to the little girl, the child, scissors in hand with the points pointing back, suddenly jerked her hand backward and jabbed the cat directly in her right eye.

The terrifyingly loud yowl from the cat and the scream from the child caused the child's mother to drop the phone and come dashing into the room. The cat, in total agony, had fled back to the other room, droplets of blood marking her trail. The child, still seated on the floor, was covered in blood and had several scratch marks on her face and arm, but the blood was mostly from the stab wound she had inflicted upon the cat. It was horrific!

The mom snatched her daughter up into her arms and ran into the kitchen, where she carefully washed away the blood and cleaned the wounds with soap and water. The injuries were not nearly as bad as she'd first imagined. Next, she got some liquid antibiotic and dressed the scratches. Although the child kicked and cried, the mom persisted, knowing that what she was doing was necessary to stave off infection. After the antibiotic was applied, the scratches stopped bleeding and did not need bandaging; she picked up her daughter and quickly returned to the room.

"What on earth could have possessed my beautiful Vivianna to scratch my baby like that?" she asked herself. In crossing the floor, she stepped on the scissors, which were under some scraps of paper. When she bent down to pick them up, she was horrified to see how bloody they were.

"Oh my God," she blurted as she looked wildly around for the cat. She put down the toddler, who had started to cry again at her mother's outburst, and told her to stay put. "Mommy will be right back." Then she went into the adjacent room to find her cat.

Vivianna was hiding in the far corner of the room behind a chair. She was terrified, bloody, and in excruciating pain. As the mother reached down to get her Vivianna tried to flee, but the lady was quick and nabbed her. When the mother picked her up she saw the eye; it was an awful sight. The orb was hanging out of the socket on the front of her face. The eyeball had been punctured; its contents poured out mingling with the blood, making a terrible, sticky mess.

Afraid that if she let go of the cat she wouldn't find her again, she went to get the carrier with the cat still in her arms. Using just one hand, she set the carrier on the first available flat surface, opened the door, and tried to push the cat inside. Vivianna was having none of it and resisted with all four paws braced against the sides of the door. In desperation the lady reset the carrier on its end with the opening to the top; holding Vivianna by the scruff of her neck, she slid her into the carrier backward. It worked! She quickly closed and latched the door before the cat realized where she was.

The lady grabbed her purse and keys, picked up her baby, took her to the car, and fastened her into her car seat. She then went back into the house for the cat carrier and her cell phone. Because she had the vet's number on speed dial, she was able to place a call at the first red light. She informed them they were on the way with an emergency situation before hanging up and driving on.

Even before she talked to the veterinarian, the woman had figured the course of treatment would be to remove the eye, and she was correct. The eye was too badly damaged to save. The surgery would be done right away to prevent any more blood loss. The veterinarian was curious as to how the cat had sustained such a traumatic injury.

"I think my daughter stabbed her in the eye with a pair of scissors," the lady said, choking back tears. "My baby was scratched on her face and arm, as you can see." She gently turned her daughter's face up with her hand under her chin so the veterinarian could look at her. "Vivianna only reacted in self-defense. She's never done anything like this before. Even when we first brought my daughter home from the hospital and put her in the crib, Vivianna would get in with her and snuggle up beside her. We've trusted Vivianna completely."

She left Vivianna at the vet's overnight so the staff could check the surgery site to make sure all was OK and draining properly. She was to pick the cat up anytime after nine the next morning.

Before the child's father got home from work, she cleaned both rooms and picked up and put away the scrapbook materials. She was almost finished getting supper ready when her husband called her into the living room.

"What in Sam Hill happened to my baby?" he demanded. "Look at her face. What happened?"

"Vivianna scratched her," said his wife meekly.

"Vivianna? What the hell . . . Where is that cat? I'll kill her!"

For the third time, the child began to wail.

"She's at the vet's. Your daughter stabbed her in the eye with my scissors and ruptured her eyeball. It couldn't be saved, so the veterinarian removed her eye. I'm to pick her up tomorrow," she spat back. It wasn't Vivianna's fault, and she was determined to stand up for her.

"You'll do nothing of the kind! She scratched my baby's face and could have put her eye out too. I'll not have that damn cat in my house. Tomorrow you'll go to the vet, pay the bill, and tell them to do whatever they want with the cat, and that's final!"

The woman did as she was told. She didn't want to bring the cat home only to have her husband kill it. At the vet's office, when the veterinarian came in to explain what was done during the surgery, she told him she couldn't take the cat home and why. She wondered if he would be so kind as to find Vivianna a good home; the vet agreed to do what he could. She asked to see her cat for the last time and spent several minutes trying to explain what had happened and why she wouldn't be taking her home; she talked to Vivianna as if she were a person. Then she paid the bill and left, heartbroken.

The veterinarian had his receptionist call a cat rescue, the same operation they'd called to pick up Shadow. As before, the director came, this time for Vivianna. He took her back to the shelter, tending her wound there until it was completely healed. Then, along with an assortment of other cats from the shelter, he brought her to the cat adoption day event.

Vivianna had become extremely angry and deeply resentful given the trauma she had endured; she didn't want human contact in any shape or form. She had suffered great pain and lost an eye and her family all in one day; none of it was even remotely her fault. Why should she trust anyone when all the people she had known and cared about had abandoned her? Unfortunately, she turned a cold shoulder to all the interested potential adopters that might have given her a good home.

Maggie and Draya had stopped by the cat adoption event to purchase bulk kitty litter that was on sale at the store. Before they went to fill up the pails, they stopped to visit their friends who had cats up for adoption. Maggie, who was "just looking," spotted Vivianna. She was captivated by Vivianna's one large pumpkin-colored eye. She told Draya that Vivianna reminded her of a pirate; all she needed was a hat and an eye patch. Their friend, the director of the shelter, told Maggie that due to her unsocial demeanor she would be very hard to place unless just the right person—someone who knew about the personality characteristics of Persian cats—would be willing to try to rehabilitate her.

Today Vivianna is enjoying her home with Maggie. She has lost a good bit of her haughtiness and fear and sleeps snuggled up as close to Maggie as she can get. The two of us have whiled away many hours in the patches of sunshine that filter in through the front room windows of Maggie's house. We have swapped lies and recanted stories about our pasts. It is amazing what can be learned if one is willing to listen.

Vivianna

Chapter 17
What's in a Name?

MAGGIE IS OFTEN asked how she comes up with the names she gives her cats. As in my case, she took into account unique personality traits. She thought me talkative, a trait she attributes to most senators, so I became "Senator." The "Bollweevil" part, as I have already said, came from Harry.

A gracious plenty of the cats and kittens that she's fostered over the years were named before she acquired them, and Maggie saw no reason to change a name they were used to being called. Annie, Shadow, Tinkerbell, and Vivianna, are more recent examples of this case.

Others she named just for the fun of it. There was "Busybritches," a cat that was always into everything; he died unexpectedly soon after I came to the neighborhood. "Toe White," a dark tortoiseshell, has one white toe on her hind paw. And, of course, my lovely "Fuzzbucket," who would get all fuzzed up at the drop of a hat.

Most of the Siamese cats she's adopted over the years were named based on Maggie's reaction to her coworkers' opinions, some of whom thought that to have more than two cats was too many to have at one time. A few even went so far as to say that having two cats at any time was two too many. So the first Siamese kitten she acquired became "So What," as in, if she got another kitten, it was not anyone's business but her own. "Why Not" was one of the three litter brothers who were brought to Draya to raise. Since Maggie had just taken on So What, it was thought that another kitten would be a good companion for him as the two were approximately the same age. "Oh, why not," Maggie had giggled. She just loved kittens.

Why Not is now a fully grown cat who curiously wouldn't use a scratching post, or the furniture (thankfully), nor any of the many trees in Maggie's backyard, like other cats would. It was a trait that Maggie hadn't noticed until he started limping on his front paw, which had apparently become quite sore; he would not let her inspect it. She finally shoved him into a carrier and took him to the vet. Upon examination, it was discovered that one of his claws had grown into the pad and the paw had begun to swell. Cats are particularly good at hiding pain or illness, so Maggie had no notion of when the injury occurred.

The vet said, "When a cat doesn't scratch and flake off the cellulose that forms around the nail, it can cause the claw to curve under. If it's not trimmed correctly, the claw will grow into the pad."

He used special nail clippers to cut the claw almost down to the quick, then removed the embedded sharp part of the claw. The puncture was deep and bled profusely. Why Not was given antibiotics and sent to Draya's to be confined in a crate until the wound healed.

Keeping the paw clean was a must, so Draya switched him to paper litter. But after two days she noticed that his foot was still swollen and needed further attention. It required surgery to clean the pus pocket that had formed. With a dose of stronger antibiotics and another week and a half in the crate, the paw healed and the claw showed signs of retracting normally, signifying success. Why Not is a lucky cat to have such a caring owner.

Draya was tickled pink to return him to Maggie's house and watch him scamper around like a kitten. She often goes next door to visit Maggie's cats and can be seen covered with cats if she sits down in one of the recliners. It's a "Pet me, pet me, pet me" situation.

Some time later, Maggie became aware of two male Siamese littermates that required a special-needs home. One had chronic intestinal problems and the other a misplaced rectum; both had severe diarrhea. It took Maggie months and many trips to the vet to alleviate their diarrhea, but for a time it went away. The cats were named "OME" and "OMI," as in, "Oh me, oh my, what have I gotten into now?"

Unfortunately, OMI's diarrhea problem became recurring and developed into chronic irritable bowel syndrome (IBS). He lost weight and could not control himself. Over the months Maggie and her veterinarians had run every test and tried every drug they knew to treat his condition. It seemed they'd run out of options. In a last ditch effort, they took him off all medication to try a special food diet.

Draya kept him crated at her house under strict observation, but to no avail. In the last week, OMI was so uncomfortable using the kitty box he cried when he pooped. They realized that his quality of life was severely diminished and his recovery unlikely. So at the tender age of nine, OMI was mercifully put to sleep. It was a sad day for Maggie and Draya. They lovingly placed OMI's remains in our kitty cemetery. I watched from the cat enclosure behind Draya's house as Maggie and Draya filled in the grave where they'd buried him. His troubles behind him, OMI crossed over the Rainbow Bridge to join the group waiting to welcome him.

Several years ago, Maggie adopted what was to be the last kitten she'd decided to welcome into her home. The kitten was not Siamese, but he was the cutest little charcoal gray and white "tuxedo" kitten I ever saw. Maggie had no hesitation at all naming him "Nomo," for obvious reasons.

Many years and many cats have come and gone; some were just passing through, some are still with her, and many have passed on. Of the myriad cat lives that Maggie has touched, some have reached the status of personal favorites. I'd like to think that I've been so lucky to earn the status of "favorite." I know one thing for sure, regardless of what the others might have aspired to, I have outlived most of them. I'm a survivor.

Chapter 18
Don't Get Caught Singing the Blues

I WROTE THIS chapter to cover some—but by no means all—of the potentially dangerous things that can cause illness, trauma, toxicity, and death to pets, and may result in expensive treatments for us as well as anguish for our owners. Years ago Gabby told me, "I didn't lick this information up off of the grass!" Well, neither did I. What I know is an accumulation of facts that I've heard or been a party to over my lifetime. It's not my intention to bore or offend my readers, but to inform cat owners, potential owners, and pet-sitters of some of the dangers and problems that exist so they may hopefully avoid issues by being proactive rather than reactive.

If you prefer not to know these potential threats, then by all means skip this chapter and go to the next one. But by doing so, you're emulating the ostrich by sticking your head in the sand. Personally, I prefer to be forewarned and therefore forearmed. Disconcerting as this information is, please keep in mind that not all pets will be confronted with many of these hazards. The luckiest ones will never face any of them. So please read on. I'll try to be brief. (If you'd like more detailed information there are numerous books available, and, of course, as Draya says, "there's the internet." Discussing issues with your veterinarian is often the best bet.)

Household cleaners, particularly those used at full strength or just slightly diluted, can cause serious problems especially if the pet is allowed to walk on surfaces that are still wet from being cleaned. Letting it dry is of particular importance with cats, as cats clean their paws by licking them and can ingest enough chemicals to poison them. Toilet bowl cleaners, especially the ones hung in the bowl or water closet to mix into the water, can kill if your animal is in the habit of drinking from the toilet bowl. Symptoms include drooling, vomiting, staggering, lethargy, and rapid breathing.

If you're in the habit of changing or adding antifreeze (ethylene glycol) to your automobile, be very sure to clean up any spills, even those that occur on dirt or gravel surfaces. Animals are drawn to the sweet smell and taste of antifreeze and will often try to lap it up wherever they find it. Just one tablespoon of it can kill a cat. It's vital to be aware of your neighbors' habits as well. If you suspect antifreeze or chemical poisoning, take the animal to a veterinarian immediately. In treating a case like this, time is of the essence.

Food allergies are more likely to cause discomfort than anything life threatening: itching, hives, watery eyes, diarrhea, vomiting. If left unchecked for extended periods of time, the symptoms will become increasingly hard to treat. Discuss them with your veterinarian when they first occur. He may be able to suggest a change in diet that will solve the problem. Many cats are or may become lactose intolerant; if so, don't feed them milk products, including yogurt or cottage cheese.

Also, never give aspirin or aspirin-like medicines (like Pepto Bismol) to cats. These compounds can cause irreversible bloody diarrhea, which can lead to death.

Strangulation and suffocation occur in many houses not only to human babies but pets as well. Cats are particularly at risk of death by strangulation via the looped cords on draperies and Venetian blinds. A lack of oxygen for as little as three to four minutes can cause brain damage. Partial strangulation can lead to an animal developing breathing and heart problems or even pulmonary edema (fluid in the lungs). A simple preventive measure is to cut the cord at the bottom of the loop and tie a knot at each end so that it won't unravel.

Suffocation frequently occurs when plastic grocery or cleaner bags are played with. Toxic fumes and a foreign body stuck in the throat can also cause an animal to suffocate. All of these situations generally require a speedy trip to the veterinarian.

Strange as it may seem, many cats are maimed in clothes dryers. Dryers are a warm, inviting spot for a nap; unless the person operating a dryer looks inside carefully before closing the door and turning it on, they might not know the cat is inside until it's too late. A cat in this situation is usually too busy trying to keep upright to call out for help, resulting in a battered, bruised cat suffering from heat stroke—if it's fortunate enough to have survived the physical trauma and extreme heat. The best prevention is to keep the dryer door closed except to load or unload and to look inside every time before turning on the dryer. Better to be safe than sorry.

I could go on, but I think you get my drift. Be aware of potential dangers before accidents occur. If you must, make a trip around the house and write down possible hazards; eliminate them if you can. If you can't eliminate them entirely, then you can at least try to do something to lessen the risks. There is no time like the present to promote safety.

In the summer months, there are a variety of hazards to animals. Fleas and ticks are far more prevalent at that time and pet owners should administer a recommended treatment monthly. A word of caution: never, ever use a treatment intended for a dog on a cat. Some of the chemicals in the treatment are easily tolerated by dogs but will kill a cat. The effects are usually irreversible: serious illness or death.

If you own a cat and a dog, do yourself a favor and write CAT and DOG in bold marker on the respective boxes. The packaging is so much alike that mixing up feline and canine doses happens more frequently than you would think. It's downright scary. The same applies to most of the liquid topical medications as well as flea and tick collars. Although widely used, I wouldn't recommend flea collars for cats. Our skin is sensitive and prone to chemical burns. Flea collars are not breakaway and last for years; plus, they are potential choking hazards.

I remember a kitten that ran away from home with a flea collar on. Several months later he was found half-starved, staggering around a parking deck gasping for breath. He had outgrown the collar and could not get it off. His rescuers took him to a vet clinic where they cut the embedded collar out of the crease in his neck. They saved the cat, but permanent damage had been done to his esophagus. That cat never meowed again; he could only squeak, which is a very strange noise coming from a cat.

Once when Maggie and Draya had taken me to our vet to get a shot for my arthritis and a shot of vitamin B-12 to help my old body better absorb the nutrients in my food, a lady came running into the office with a limp cat in her arms. It was a blisteringly hot day, almost 92 degrees Fahrenheit. The woman was sobbing and muttering something to the receptionist. Never one to ignore a story, I listened intently.

"I was on my way here for Archie's annual checkup and shots, but I had to stop at the pharmacy for a refill on my medicine," she stammered through tears of anguish. "I cracked all the windows as low as I could without Archie being able to get out. I was only in the pharmacy a few minutes to pick up my prescription and pay for it. I went straight to the car, but when I got there, Archie was lying on his side on the front seat.

"It was so hot in the car when I got in that I started it right away to get the air-conditioner going. I couldn't get Archie to get up. He just lay there like a limp dishrag. I came here as fast as I dared," she said, talking to anyone who was listening.

Halfway through her story, the veterinarian and his assistant came rushing into the reception area and took Archie out of her arms and headed back to surgery, where they immediately wrapped him in cold, wet towels, placed ice packs on his chest and groin areas, and started IV fluids. They paid particular attention to cooling his head, neck, and the pads of his paws. They took his temperature every ten minutes to determine how high it was and if it was coming down.

Cats and dogs don't perspire as humans do, and cats don't pant as efficiently as dogs. Brain damage can occur when a cat's body temperature reaches 106 or 107 degrees Fahrenheit for any length of time. Death can occur if the temperature isn't lowered quickly.

Fortunately, Archie received treatment in the nick of time. His temperature returned to normal, and he recovered fully after several days of rest. I appreciated Maggie's follow-up to me on what had happened. She saw how concerned I was while we were still in the waiting room; true to her fashion, Maggie attempted to explain all of it to me—just as if I was a person—when we got home.

I was also impressed that none of the other caregivers at the vet's that morning were upset about having to wait a little beyond their scheduled appointment time while Archie was being treated. The veterinarian took the time to come out and explain some of the warning signs of heatstroke to everyone in the waiting room. The signs include warm foot pads, glazed eyes, heavy panting, rapid pulse, dark red or purple tongue, high body temperature, dizziness, vomiting, and diarrhea. He emphasized the risks of keeping pets in a hot car and how quickly the temperature can rise inside a car, even with the windows all the way down. Animals confined to carriers are more at risk due to the minimized air circulation in the carrier. In the direct sun, a carrier can become an oven. The vet thanked everyone for having patience and then called in his next client.

Stings from bees, caterpillars, and scorpions, and bites from snakes, spiders, mosquitoes, and flies are other summertime hazards. Cats that travel with their caregivers around the country are very susceptible to the natural dangers that exist outside of their comfort zone. Deer ticks carry Lyme disease, and mosquitoes carry heartworm microfilaria, which is an increasing problem throughout the United States. It's easily spread to other animals when animals infected with heartworm microfilaria return to areas not previously affected by the pathogens. Bee and other stings, while usually just painful, can also trigger allergic reactions, but scorpion stings and snake and spider bites can sometimes be lethal.

There are enough plants out there that are highly toxic to cats and dogs for me to write a book on the subject. Obviously, some may be more toxic than others, but most will typically cause some digestive upset. A case in point is grass; we cats eat it as a spring/summer tonic to help us rid our stomachs of foreign materials such as hair ingested while grooming—or whatever has looked interesting enough to pick up in our mouths and swallow. It's a perfectly natural thing for us to do, no matter how unpleasant it is for our caregivers to clean up. The problem comes when we move on to nibbling on other plants, some of which can wreak disastrous results if eaten.

According to Draya, there are many websites that list dozens of poisonous plants and give the symptoms of each, if one is curious enough to look them up. Lilies are among the most toxic plants of all to cats, including tiger lilies, daylilies, Easter lilies, Stargazer lilies, Japanese show lilies, wood lilies, and Rubrum lilies. Ingesting even two to three petals or leaves can result in kidney failure and death.

There are many other plants just as lethal. Thankfully, most are usually grown outside and pose little threat to an indoor-only cat. But plants that are brought inside in dish gardens or pots can be very dangerous to greenery-starved indoor cats. If you must have the plants inside, please try to make them as inaccessible as possible. Remember, cats are agile and can climb almost anything. Try to make informed decisions as to which plants to bring in and which are best admired outside; it may well save your cat's life. If you suspect your cat has ingested a poisonous plant, take your cat to the veterinarian ASAP. If you are unsure of the name of the plant, take the plant or a portion of it with you; its identification will help the vet quickly diagnose and treat your pet.

Just as plants can be toxic, so can the pesticides, fungicides, and herbicides used in abundance to enhance yards and gardens in both urban and rural areas. When first applied and still wet (or powdery), these chemicals can be picked up on paws with terrible consequences. Keep in mind that those chemicals are created to kill, and they're very effective at doing just that.

Enough said. Please practice awareness.

Now, where's Draya? I need my midnight snack.

Chapter 19
Lifesavers Come in All Shapes

As Miss G and Harry became less able to care for themselves, their daughter Jan came to live with them. Jan, who grew up as a child in our neighborhood, had just retired. She had two cats of her own that she brought into the family. I certainly didn't mind having new sisters. I had no recollection of my siblings; it had been too many years. I left it totally up to the new girls as to whether they liked me or not. It took time, but my advancing age and laid-back attitude finally won them over; at least I think it did.

Miss G was delighted to have her daughter home, though as long as Miss G was physically able, she still wanted to cook and help with the housework. Her eyes were beginning to cloud, and she didn't see so well anymore. Nonetheless, she was cut from a remarkable bolt of cloth, and even into her early nineties she still took care of her flower gardens. I took every step that she took; we were a great team, the two of us.

Miss G knew that my favorite meal was boiled chicken, and she fixed it for me as often as she could. She was very careful, as usual, to remove all the bones. But one day she was distracted while fixing the chicken for me and she missed a few bones. Unfortunately, cooked chicken bones are very brittle, and when broken can be quite sharp. I ate the plate of chicken with my usual gusto and licked the platter clean. A short time later I developed a cough, small at first, but it grew steadily. It sounded as though I was ridding my system of a hairball, but it felt different. Something had lodged in my throat.

Miss G had become frail enough to require a caregiving companion for several hours a day. The arrangement allowed Jan a respite during the day to shop, take a class at the local university, or attend a program she wanted to see. With her companion, Miss G was still able to go on short walks using a walker. I felt it my duty to accompany her wherever she went. Sick and frail by this point myself, I could only go part of the way on her walk. I'd sit down on the side of the street and wait for her to return so we could walk back to the house together. I knew she was very worried about me; she talked it over with Jan often.

Everyone at our house thought I was probably just suffering from a hairball or a pollen allergy. So they pretty much ignored the issue, trusting it would go away on its own; it did not. After enough time had passed, irritation caused the tissue in my throat to thicken, and eventually it formed a cyst. It wasn't discovered until I went to the vet for my annual vaccinations. The veterinarian was amazed at the size of the cyst. According to him, it had become almost impossible for me to eat or breathe. I had lost nearly two pounds and had developed an audible wheeze. He speculated it might be a tumor of the thyroid gland, but my blood work indicated that it wasn't. He recommended I be taken to a specialist.

Shortly after my visit to the vet's office, I was placed in a carrier and loaded into Draya's car. Maggie was there with us. We drove and drove and drove. It seemed to me we would never get to where we were going. Finally, we arrived at our destination, a specialty hospital where they ran tests to determine whether the cyst was a tumor and whether it involved the thyroid gland. Was the condition operable? Was I strong enough to undergo surgery? Several hours later it was decided that one of their surgeons would try to remove it. They wouldn't be able to tell how much the surgery would involve until they opened up the area. My blood work revealed that the cyst was starting to become cancerous; the only options left were surgery or euthanasia.

Speaking by phone, Jan made the call to do the surgery. I was her mom's favorite cat, and she wanted to save me if at all possible. I certainly was relieved and grateful to hear her decision.

Due to the heavy schedule at the hospital, the surgery wasn't scheduled until the following week. Maggie and Draya agreed to bring me home and drive down again for the surgery. In the meantime, I was to stay at Draya's house. She could confine me in a large cat crate until we returned for my surgery. It was meant to keep me out of any further trouble I might get into outside, as well as help her locate me when she needed to give me antibiotics.

It was important that I had plenty of small meals that would be easier for me to swallow. The night before my scheduled surgery I wasn't allowed to eat anything after supper. I was allowed water until morning, but by then my throat had closed so much I didn't feel like eating or drinking anything anyway.

Draya was kind enough to set up a portable crate complete with water and food bowls should I need them later, and a clean litter box. I had long since gotten over my aversion to an inside litter pan. No food was offered, but a small amount of water was there if I needed it. To make sure my ride down and back would be comfortable she placed a folded towel on the floor of the crate with a padded kitty cozy on top of the towel. No matter the outcome of the day, I was going in style!

We arrived at the clinic in a timely fashion, and because my surgery was slated so early, I didn't have long to wait. A few questions were asked and answered then I was whisked away to meet my destiny. Maggie and Draya were to wait until the surgery was completed and I became fully awake. At that time it would be decided if I could go home or should stay overnight.

The surgery completed, the surgeon went out to talk with Maggie and Draya. After careful consideration, and his being assured that I would be confined to a clean, comfortable crate (not allowed to mingle with the other cats in the house, or let outside until my incision had a chance to heal), the surgeon agreed to allow Draya to take me to her home for my recovery period. They were instructed to call the hospital if needed; if not, he would see me for a recheck in two weeks.

When the technician returned me in my carrier to Maggie and Draya, they were still talking to my surgeon. Through sleepy, blurry eyes I was relieved to see smiles all around. According to what the doctor said next, my surgery should be a complete success. He was able to remove the entire mass and from what he saw there was no indication of any involvement with the thyroid gland. Yippee!

Pausing for a moment, he looked puzzled. "With all the animals I know you have worked with during the years, how in the world did Senator get a bone fragment lodged in his throat and no one suspect it?"

"A bone fragment?" they both uttered in the same breath. "I have no idea," Maggie said, clearly puzzled.

"Wait a minute," Draya said. "Don't you remember Jan calling me to ask if chicken bones were dangerous to cats? I told her they were, cooked ones especially because they're so brittle and prone to splintering. I think it was while Senator was still living at Miss G's. Now that I think about it, it was at about the same time you noticed his cough, which I thought was probably due to the pollen last spring."

Draya looked the surgeon square in the eye and said, "We know that Miss G cooked a chicken for him once a week, but I'm positive she always deboned it very carefully." She was very matter-of-fact about it.

"You don't suppose her failing eyesight caused her to miss one or two?" Maggie said as she knit her eyebrows together and tried to remember things that Jan had shared with her about her mother's failing health. "If he did ingest a bone while he was there, it was by sheer mistake. Miss G was always so careful when it came to Senator."

Draya agreed. "I think the cause wasn't picked up by our vets at home because everyone was thinking thyroid tumor; the mass was so darn close to the gland. Without further testing, they couldn't know for sure. That was why they sent us here for diagnostics."

I, on the other hand, still groggy from the anesthetic, was beginning to realize how completely famished I was. Having had nothing to eat since supper brought that long subdued feeling of homelessness and uncertainty I'd felt when I ran away from my first home years and years ago. I was perplexed that such a deep-seated emotion became accessible under the right circumstances. But never being one to dwell on the past I addressed the situation at hand. "Meow," I said. "Meow, meow, meow." I was very tired, thirsty, and hungry.

"Sounds like your boy is wide awake now and probably hungry," said the surgeon. "Feed him lightly, just small amounts every two to three hours for several days. If his appetite is good, and I imagine it will be, you can increase his feeding to the normal amounts. You can even supplement his food with vitamins to help him gain back some of the weight he lost during his ordeal.

"I think he'll do well now. The mass was just a cyst that had formed around the bone fragment. In truth, the cyst probably saved his life by preventing the sharp end of the bone from further penetrating his esophagus or trachea. He's a lucky cat to have owners who care enough to invest the time and money to save him." The surgeon seemed impressed.

During the car ride home, I was offered small sips of water and small amounts of wet cat food, which I gratefully and carefully consumed. I almost felt like I had to learn to swallow all over again. Maybe I did, or maybe I didn't, but fortunately the feeling passed quickly, and I was back on my regular feeding schedule in no time—back home safe and sound.

My follow-up appointment involved blood work to determine if any cancer cells were still present. My incision had healed rapidly for a cat my age, and I had put on some much-needed weight. My surgeon was delighted to report no more cancer cells had been detected, so relatively speaking I was as good as new. Everyone breathed a huge sigh of relief, especially me.

Sadly, shortly after my surgery, while I was convalescing in the crate at Draya's house, my beloved Miss G passed away due to complications resulting from a fall. We were all grieved to lose such a dear, caring, and well-loved member of our community. Miss G was a true friend to those who knew her well. I miss her so much that when Jan comes to visit Draya, I am drawn immediately to her; she sounds so much like her mom. I'm compelled to sit near her and have her pet me. If I were allowed, I'd accompany Jan home and look for Miss G myself; I just can't believe she's actually gone.

The consensus among my caregivers mandated that I become an indoor-only cat. Considering all of the vet bills that had been paid on my behalf, it would make me a very expensive "flat cat" if I were to be hit by a car or truck.

I must admit that the pros of living indoors do outweigh the cons: it's warm and dry in winter and cool and secure in summer; there are clean litter boxes in private places around the house, fresh cool drinking water, and food for the asking. My journey has been long and at times arduous. I have arthritis in my back and still don't absorb all the nutrition I need from food, so I get a vitamin B-12 shot every month. My hearing's less sharp, but some of it I'd lost before I was brought inside. Oh, and I'm sure I don't see everything I think I see, but all in all, I'm happy and content.

I enjoy going out into Draya's securely fenced backyard, including the patio and deck for soaking up the sun, and there's always the koi pond for entertainment. My outdoor buddies, Stranger and William Wallace, now live here too. We can come and go at will, day or night, out to the deck into the backyard enclosure through a sheltered cat door set in a window. It's an arrangement we all enjoy.

I went from being a kitten of questionable heritage to being possibly the most expensive cat in the neighborhood, and I never once let it go to my head. I was, and fortunately still am, Senator Bollweevil, cat extraordinaire!

Epilogue

I F I'VE ERRED by using too many clichés, please don't be harsh in your judgment of me. Please take into consideration that I'm a cat with a vocabulary limited to what I've heard from the "cat-speak" of felines I've known throughout the years, in addition to what the people around me have said. Both my advanced age and keen desire to learn—or at least listen and retain facts and phrases—have allowed me to glean a fair amount of information not usually associated with cats, regardless of how smart we truly are.

My intention throughout this book has been to inform my readers and make them aware of some of the issues pertinent to cats in particular, and in certain cases other pets that also might be affected. Depending upon what might happen to a cat, the "nine lives" attributed to us can be significantly tested. I consider myself to be one of the lucky ones.

S. B.

***

To say what you want is one thing.
To want what you say is another.
My advice for today
Is mean what you say,
And print it for someone else to discover.

A. H. L.